BAILEY

GIULIANO BRIGANTI   JOHN HOLLANDER

WILLIAM BAILEY

RIZZOLI
NEW YORK

First published in the United States of America in 1991 by
RIZZOLI INTERNATIONAL PUBLICATIONS, INC.
300 Park Avenue South, New York, NY 10010

Photography by:
Alfio Di Bella, Rome
Eeva Inkeri, New York
John D. Schiff, New York
Scheenen & Junger
Robert Waddel
Allan Finkelman
Rolly Marchi, Milan
Sandro Manzo, Rome
Fm Marchese di C.G., Milan
Paola Gribaudo, Turin

ISBN 0-8478-1345-2
LC 90/63627

Designed and edited by Paola Gribaudo

English language translation by Peter Glendening
and Maria Fitzgerald

Printed in Italy by
Stamperia Artistica Nazionale - Turin

CONTENTS

Can we understand better the meaning of an artist's work by knowing him personally? Yes and no. I could say I hardly know William Bailey. I met him only once, in Rome, where at the Calcografia Nazionale many of his paintings and drawings were in an exhibition; a few words exchanged in the span of a few minutes, standing in the midst of the noisy and distracted crowd that usually attends the openings: words of admiration on my part, words of thanks on his (I had been the organizer of the exhibition) and that was all. Very little, hardly anything.

But I recall the impression made on me by the gentle reserve of a man of few words and few gestures, the slightly studied and detached attitude of a scientist or of a man of religion, the smile acting more as a defence than an invitation to a dialogue. In that smile I discerned his hesitation to break out of a long habit of silence and solitude, as if fearing a lack of total and immediate consensus to conclusions which he found unquestionable, and which had led him to work slowly and introspectively. Or rather, as if he thought that the real sense of his work lay only in his long and thoughtful artistic apprenticeship, in the cultivation of his eye the true result would be his own vision of things. Very difficult to translate into words such a path and such a goal.

The silence that emanates from his paintings, does it not perhaps in its own turn recall silence? Though I live a visual life, I have difficulties on the subject, I have my reservations as to the possibility of approaching the formal value of paintings through words. Especially if the pure visual values are dominant as in Bailey. So dominant, that I cannot even now tell whether my impression of that short exchange, and his impression on me might not have stemmed solely from what I had been seeing in his work. This would reverse the terms of the question I put to myself at the beginning: the paintings help us to understand what the artist is like in real life and not the other way around.

His paintings and drawings return my gaze metaphors of silence. Their formal message is intense; an intensity which reaches its peak in some of the still-life drawings.

No part of the surface, with its uninterrupted pattern of connections, remains inert to a sensibility trained to perceive the life of forms and to know their values. I look at those drawings, those paintings and I realize that I don't care if I know almost nothing about what their author might have said about them, no more than what little I have read in various writings on the subject. I don't care if I don't know with what spirit, with what travail, with what uncertainties and with what revelations he has ventured down the long road, which from the beginning lead him to paint and draw in the style that now is his and only his.

I can only suppose that he has had a difficult formation, not only difficult but solitary. I think of how he moved from early experiments to the achievements of today, on the impulse of a youthful vocation for drawing, which took him from art school in the Midwest to experiences in the Korean war, to Yale and to studies with Josef Albers. I don't know what the old teacher of the Bauhaus could have taught him, except perhaps a general habit of rigour, nor do I know what effect the work of American abstract Expressionists could have had on him, from Pollock to De Kooning, whom he certainly knew already at Yale. It is easier to imagine the nature of his feeling for the past, as he repeatedly looked at the classics of European painting. The basket of fruit by Caravaggio in the Ambrosian, and the hieratic still-lifes by Zurbarán are often cited in this connection. They are certainly a point of reference in his wide search for a formal vocabulary, together with others in Mediterranean culture.

I look at works spanning the last twenty years, I look at his portraits of girls and his nudes, who definitely exclude any possibility of narrative in painting but enclose reality within the confines suggested by a remote formal instinct, an instinct which is apparently innate but which in the artist's eye manages to find its roots and through them to manipulate reality. I look at his still-lifes (so often with suggestive Italian titles, at those distinct domestic objects arranged frontally on top of a table that coincides with the line of the horizon. They stand against a barely modulated background with the studied conventional equilibrium of sculpture on the pediment of a Greek temple or the sacrality of objects set out on an altar. I gaze at them, these works of art, and it seems to me that they, in their mute discreet language, in their reticent clarity, tell me everything that is worth knowing about them, if "knowing" is the right verb to use; or rather, all that I can understand by looking. In them I perceive an obscure and tenacious desire to take possession of things; of those things that, among the many that the world offers him, lend themselves to being constructed with the artist's eye (if I'm not wrong, it is his own expression), i.e. to be fashioned with the formal hallmark that his mind has constructed, drawn from the remote origins of the norm. That is to say, drawn from the law that governs the musical harmony of forms, which I imagine Bailey understands as something very similar to the mythical harmony of the celestial spheres. A formal norm with its own history. The particularity of his feeling for the past consists in searching for it and showing it to be relevant. Because in this century which spent its first years in a violent war against the past and, during its course, has always renewed and renews again what is still called the avant-garde spirit, William Bailey picks up again tenaciously and full of faith the threads of a visual concern, of an aspect of the life of forms, that takes place over a long period of time and that runs as a current beneath the surface of contemporary art, emerging sometimes as a desire for order and formal beauty, even in contemporary expressions seemingly most in revolt against the past.

In Bailey this formal aspect manifests itself as an explicit reference to historical sources, mainly in the need to fill the emptiness of space with the fullness of objects and with the fullness of space between objects through the severe dialectic of formal relations.
A denial of space being empty, which has its origin in Piero della Francesca's perspective synthesis. Significantly Bailey has titled one of his most beautiful paintings ''Monterchi'' still-life.

Giuliano Briganti

Translated by Peter Glendening

Bailey 1984

1. *Double self-portrait,* 1984

There are many kinds of painting, and in coming to discursive terms with the work of a painter who pursues one or two "kinds" of picture in a relentless and continuing quest, one has to understand how sub-types develop and proliferate and revise previous ones. In a crude sense, William Bailey's work is of two kinds: there are paintings of things without people, and paintings of nude women with few objects in them. This is perhaps to get something very wrong about both his nudes and his still lifes. And yet there is also something very right about it and what, construed more profoundly, it might mean. But other false agendas which tend to clamor for attention when his work is discussed are far noisier. The hard-rock rant of the issue of "realism" is one of these; the saccharine ballad of the "poetic" is another. But in trying to characterize the ways in which Bailey's work is and is not abstract, or the peculiar character of light, shadow and tonality in his paintings and what kind of fictive world they help create, the language of easy journalism will not do.

Writing of painting is dangerous at best, partially because the strongest interpretation of a painting is often another painting, by another artist who has seen something that the original arist has done and perhaps not even "seen" himself. "In writing," wrote William Hazlitt, "you have to contend with the world; in painting, you have only to carry on a friendly strife with Nature." True enough, if it is always remembered that the art of the past is for a true artist, part of Nature. "Things seen are things as seen" said Wallace Stevens, thereby asking us always to think of how only in painting, perhaps, can the splendid matter of that "as" be made visible. But for painting things are always "as have been seen" as well. And yet the consequences of this all point forward in time, and one thinks of Valéry's remark that "The painter should not paint what he sees, but what will be seen." That is, in some way or other, every true artist's painted world is always not merely visual, but visionary. And thus in trying to get something right about Bailey's art one has to contend with both Nature and the world, and to try to grasp what "things as seen by Bailey" might really consist of. Stevens' corollary observation that "realism is a corruption of reality" is of limited help here. We also have to deal with the emotional tone of Bailey's painting in the knowledge that, similarly, sentimentality is a corruption of feeling.

Bailey started out with the impulses of an abstract painter, but discovered after a European trip in 1960 that — in his own words — he "felt the greatest artistic freedom in dealing with a specific observable situation that what happened to me when I was trying to describe something was more abstract and carried more meaning that

2. *Untitled,* 1955

when I was simply trying to put something down that merely looked abstract.'' In some of his painting early in the following decade, a few minimal forms — in most instances, ovoids — provided the focus of structural and tonal concerns. And yet it was ''describing'' the specificity of actual eggs that yielded the abstracted forms of the painted objects. At Yale, he had been the student of Josef Albers, a painter concerned primarily with the relations of hues (and, at most, sharply stepped gradations of hue). The explorations of tonality throughout Bailey's works were for a long time unclouded by particular emotional character, and served more as an ordering principle and even as a generative spirit. More recently, having built a visual world in which the tonal structure generally casts everything composed in it in a meditative light, he has begun to associate emotional character — *êthos* as the Greeks called it — with particular modalities of tone. But tonality, like form, like texture, like the matter of contingent recessive space, all arise for him from the occasion of representation, which is why he has guardedly identified himself as a figurative artist.

Even the notion of "figurative" — rather than (at once more grossly and more narrowly) "realistic" — art raises profound questions. The artist himself has articulated this question with unusual effectiveness; implicitly invoking the highly complex history of the very word "figure" itself, he qualifies the visual meaning of the word (recognizable representation of person, thing and perhaps place) with the use of the word in rhetoric or poetics, to mean "non-literal." Like that of other important painters today (Leland Bell comes immediately to mind), Bailey's work is not literally, but (in that other sense) figuratively, figurative. His representations are not what he calls "descriptions," of objects but rather represent those descriptions, distanced from their objects as is the process of *dal vero* drawing from the consequences of this in his painting. This is most pointedly important in his painted nude figures, that with very few exceptions resist questions which would apply to their personhood, real or fictional.

Hazlitt, a painter as well as a writer, is again interesting here. He invokes and then misquotes John Donne's lines about the subject of his second "Anniversary" poem, to the effect that: "we understood Her by her sight; her pure and eloquent blood Spoke in her cheeks, and so distinctly wrought That one might almost say her body thought . . . "

In talking of "the slow, patient, laborious execution of Coreggio, Leonardo da Vinci and Andrea del Sarto, where every touch appears conscious of its charge, emulous of truth" (these painters were for Hazlitt as I thinks Ingres has been to Bailey) he said that "the artist has so distinctly wrought, that you might almost say his picture thought!"

And so of Bailey's nude figures: we do not wonder of them what they are thinking; we do not even infer the thoughts of their bodies, rather than their minds. But we feel the thought, the thoughtfulness, of the pictures they help compose.

Perhaps it is in regard to this figurative quality of his painted figuration that the emergence of his work in still life from a more abstract intention can be best un-

3. *Eggs,* 1966

derstood. It will be instructive in this regard to consider one of his earliest still lifes, the *Untitled* of 1966. The paintings of eggs which preceded it had all been elliptical — in that other sense of the word — in what they excluded, and in how they averted their world from all but these objects which were topologically so simple, and simply so self-contained, and perhaps even self-possessed. (Bailey indeed remembers Conrad Marca-Relli speaking to him at that time of eggs as "forms already purified"). Particularly in the *Eggs* of the same year, their placement further excludes whole orders of complication. Only one of the six eggs is partially occluded by another (and it is so much a matter of occlusion of painted form rather than of palpable touch of egg on egg), and that occluding one, central though not mid-most, lies not only across the line of join of the two pieces of fabric but with its long axis aligned with it. This central egg also bears the weight of another important matter: it is responsible for the only complex shadow form, creeping in under the fold of cloth and establishing the darkest tonal point in the painting.

But the eggs take on another conceptual dimension when introduced onto the top of a palpable table, and associated as elements of a proper *nature morte* with the fork, coffee-pot and knife. And yet the objects are set up in such an apparently simple fashion as to be extremely problematic. While the eggs are so placed that a line drawn between their "centers" (at any rate, the mid-point between their foci) roughly parallels the perspective recession of the table-edge on the (viewer's) right, the alignment of pot, fork and knife is purely rectangular when projected onto the picture plane itself. They are somewhat dumbly placed, and could be said to compose an abstract structure of a different order from that generated by the eggs-as-on-the-table, although they manage to maintain their illusionistic places on the surface, glued there by drawing and shadow.

And yet they make a subtle and powerful point about what still life painting has been, and can yet be. As such, it is something of a manifesto, not for an artistic move-

ment or moment, but an internal proclamation about Bailey's own work. The knife-handle, projecting as it does over the left-hand edge of the table, is at once alluding to and thereby turning aside from the conventional knife-handles in paintings from the Dutch to Chardin and after — from the more naively projecting handles which, as it were, invite you to pick them up and enter the illusion, to the more sophisticated ones which poke diagonally out at us to remind us emphatically that the edge of the table top is *not* on the picture plane itself. Bailey's handle refuses to be and do a number of things in a kind of series palimpsests: first, it refuses to claim to be an actual knife handle (''*Ceci n'est pas un pipe''* — but this so primitive that it almost goes without saying). Next, it refuses to enter into a typical still life narrative, answering to discursive rather than visual curiosity (''Whose table is this? By whom, and why, were just these things placed just this way? Arranged? Why? Abandoned after use? If so, in a hurry? or normally and casually?'' and so forth). Again, it refuses to be a *trompe-l'oeil* handle, extending its specter of graspability toward the viewer greedy for literal illusion. And yet again, it abjures the role of spatial indicator mentioned originally, almost saying to us ''Thank you, I prefer the fables of Mondrian,'' and preferring, if anything, to be almost at one with the verticality of the pot and fork which do in fact signal spatial recession a well as planar direction.

With further exploration of these issues during the next few years, Bailey found himself wandering into the genre of still life, although with no original intention to journey there. And here, too, the figurativeness, the metaphorically removed aim of his representation, is fully as important as it is for his figures. Some general observations about *nature morte* may be in order at this point.

* * *

Wallace Stevens once observed that "Pareto's epigram that history is a cemetery of aristocracies easily becomes another: that poetry is a cemetery of nobilities," by which he meant to point out that, just as new aristocracies supersede previous ones, new conceptions of what is noble, great, beautiful or sublime will eventually join the older conceptions — once youthful, then vigorous, and later wise — beneath the grass. So we might add that art is a cemetery not of resemblances, but of representations. In particular, the history of still life is a graveyard of the way objects can be made to look.

A painter whose work so involves a continued searching and working through of the realm of still life occasions some consideration of the nature of that realm and its immensely rich history. That history, like so many others in the worlds of art, poetry and music, involves a series of revisions of what has previously occurred, and imaginative innovations which play off prior ones. Objects of gustation or domestic use — including things which have never breathed, creatures which no longer do so, and plants which no longer grow, all "still" in different ways — surrender their images to a different nature in which they may all variously live and, unmoving, have their being. The unfolding history of how those images were derived from their objects, how they were composed, and how they inhabited, spatially and structurally, their new painted natural world, involves the successive biographies of representations. But the chronicle of what still life pictures have been variously intended to mean is another sort of story. Remembering something of both of those stories can be of help in understanding Bailey's still lifes and their relation to his vision of painting generally.

Early Hellenistic still life paintings were often called "*xenia*" or "guest" pictures, because the profusion of comestibles they depicted were those sent around to the houses of foreign visitors by their hosts of the previous evening. The third century a.d. writer Philostratus' notional description of one of these, full of detailed observations about the array of kinds and conditions of various fruits in the picture he is interpreting, nevertheless makes the issue of painting as important as that of the objects themselves from the very outset. He implies that the painted figs of the picture cry out for informed and meditative notice — which includes interpretation — just as actual ripe, juicy figs cry out to be eaten ("It's good to gather figs and also not to keep silent about the figs in this painting," he begins). Later on in this little essay he remarks of some piled-up pears and apples that "their redness has not been applied from outside but has arisen from within," which, of course, is not how actual fruit ripens, but rather the way in which depicted fruit figuratively "ripens" as layers of paint are applied. (The natural history of painted objects is an open-ended book).

Philostratus' *ekphrases* or interpretive descriptions of pictures seem to speak in part for the painter, as well as the informed viewer; for whatever the function of the *xenia* still life, whatever its role as a social commodity, for the mind and hand of the painter as for the hungry, inquiring eye of the best viewer, the parts of the painting that happen to be fruit are elements of making, not merely of betokening or reminding. Paintings are pictures (*e.g.* of fruit), rather than fruit pictured, and from this point of view, Philostratus writes like a reader of modern art.

At other times since, still life painting has been variously shadowed by different kinds of ulteriority. Late sixteenth and early seventeenth-century northern *nature morte* can be moral emblems, displaying worldly objects in all their vanity, whether accompanied or not by the human skull that cannot say, but only mean, "*memento mori,*" "remember you'll die," and, thereby, that all these elegant or ingenious or learned or expensive objects are acquired, possessed and admired (and perhaps even painted?) in vain. These are painted emblems, composed of objects individually emblematic in themselves, and assembled in ways whose visual syntax often helps to expand larger parables. But in the later seventeenth century, these give way to what is called in Dutch *pronk,* or "show-off," still life, boasting of the richness of the array of objects displayed (which is itself apparent only through the simultaneously boasted-of skill of the painter). Whatever allegories such pictures might present are inadvertent and even half-repressed historiography, of the romance of commodities, of the piety invested in the Dutch home, perhaps of wealth as moral health. The same sort of fly on a piece of fruit which might in the earlier *vanitas* painting indicate its perishability — and sometimes, at another level, the transitoriness even of frozen moments — will in a later, less morally-loaded painting, play a part in a trick of *trompe-l'oeil*. In this case, the fly will make visual claim to being a real one, attracted to the painted melon or peach by *their* illusory realism. And thus the old fable of *trompe-l'oeil* told by Pliny, of how the Greek painter Zeuxis represented a bunch of grapes so remarkably that birds flew in at the picture to consume them, is itself illustrated with a second order of illusion. But this is just more *pronk,* a final bit of joint boasting, both the painter's and that of the patron or customer who is able to afford *that* kind of workmanship. Whatever moral, whatever meaning there is, it is not the artist's, but that of the ironic tale-teller, Clio herself.

For the significance of still life in late modernity we should consider a sequence starting with Chardin that, at its outset, leaves the kinds of problem of meaning in these Dutch pictures far behind. This sequence generates a *line* here, a poetic and imaginative line, a tradition embodied in the evolution of a mythology that is not about objects in the world, but about elements of paintings. The criticism of modern art has been plagued with a literalistic notion of ''subject matter'' in much the same way that literary history and critical journalism used to be trapped in the older concept of ''theme.'' Perhaps the watershed for the question of the ''subject matter'' of still life painting is Chardin's substitution of his dear pots and pans and dead game for the grand portrait or heroic landscape or major narrative — those genres that in the eighteenth century outranked the lowly still life.

But Chardin was neither falsely modest nor a caricaturist of objects worthy of attention. What comes enclosed in his kitchen niches are almost sacral for the bourgeois *philosophe,* and become thereafter, for the history of art, heroic legends as well. There is nothing literal about Chardin's *pronk* — it is a matter of shared wonder, not praise demanded, and to that degree Chardin's paintings all teach us how to look and how to admire. There is nothing literal, too, about his painted objects and relations (What is so important is that he *does* paint the relations). For all these have become imagined — ''abstract,'' in Stevens sense of the word; that is, they are reinvented in the lengthy planning of the set-up, and refigured again in their total pictorial roles — seemingly guarding, upstaging, supporting, casting reflections or shadows upon, looking like, pointing at, attending to, serving, ignoring the other objects in the set-up. Never again would small things be the same; in particular, never would the objects being painted remain merely the ''subject'' of the picture, whether in the sense of the word used in portraiture (bowls of strawberries sitting for their portraits) or in informal discourse (as a ''topic'' or ''theme'' — what casual discourse, too often misleadingly, says a picture is ''of''). And after Cézanne began opening up the spaces of the ad hoc, and painted voids had themselves begun to enter our visual world as substances, then never again would formal relations be the same.

Both cubism and metaphysical painting privileged still life for a number of reasons, but both would shift the imaginative grounds for presentation of an ''object'' in *nature morte* even further. In the first instance for example, a recognizable representation of a pot or a guitar or a bit of newspaper would surrender its power of trivial resemblance to a higher and more authentic cause, that of the structural integrity of the entire painting, instead of merely accomodating to it. A piece of a projection of a solid object would lock into a piece of its development; shadow would evermore refuse to model, but be of one substance with what casts it and what it is cast upon; and the integrity of the still life ''pot'' or ''fabric'' of ''mandolin'' would now be understood as being complete in its refusals of the struggle to pretend to volume, as having achieved peace, as it were, of plane.

Any contemporary still life painting, then, in order to be a serious work of art

6. *Still life,* 1984

and not just an item of fashionable commodity, must imply some kind of revisionary statement *about* its genre — about still life art and what it might possibly mean. First it must declare itself and come up with a notion about what, in fact, the elements of its unique, or (in Bailey's case, putative) set-up are. Consider, for example, the following sets of elements (although existing in various visual and conceptual domains, they are all subject to painted representation in modern art):

(*a*) This table-top, these lemons, this bottle, this knife.

(*b*) This possible representational version of anything in (*a*), involving generality and specificity, scale and perspectival questions and, as always, allusion to other previous such versions.

(*c*) These patches of pigment, these moments of drawing, these passages, these gestures of the brush, these gestures of the form, these relations of hue and tone.

(*d*) These near-emblematic marks and signs that the modern eye now conjures up from among the elements of (*c*), before post-Impressionism thought not to carry significance in themselves.

(*e*) These metaphors of volume, these marriages of imagined space to almost tactile surface, these contentions of volumetric fiction and plane fact.

(*f*) These geometric or plastic structural paradigms emerging from associations of the identifiable elements of (*a*), these relations shadowed by inference, these voids and meeting-places of figure on ground, and on grounded figure, objectified in paint.

(*g*) These fables of contiguity which might push the pictured assemblage of objects in their feigned space toward the condition of landscape, or toward that of figure-group.

There are of course many, many more such sets, including a host of referential or allusive elements — the painter Gabriel Laderman observed to one of his students that one could not paint apples on a rumpled table cloth without contracting thereby to engage a particular genre that might be called "a Cézanne." That all this is so much a given of even elementary discourse about modern art. It is since Chardin that every still life painting, to be a work of art rather than merely a product of craft, must select its own unique set of elements from the elements and subsets of those like (*a*), (*b*), (*c*), etc. In other words, a contemporary still life that is not merely to be a tired replica of another artist's conception must implicitly invent a new genre. It does so partly by metaphoric revision (or *transumption,* as poetic theory calls it) of the prior notion. More specifically, it creates a new mode of object-hood (e.g. "a 1919 Morandi bottle;" "a Chirico *petit-beurre* biscuit;" "a piece of Thiebaud pie;" "a Matthiasdottir eggplant"). It also invents a new mode of relations — structural, spatial, painterly and even mythological-among those objects (e.g. they may variously generate space behind them or lock in, Vuillard-like, to their backgrounds; their own forms may be made to gesture, on the one hand, or on the other to act geometrically across the plane of the whole painting, etc.). When Chardin relates, metaphorically — by manifest form and hue and brush-stroke — and structurally, a slab of meat to a hanging piece of fabric to create a new natural taxonomy, what it means to paint objects without people visibly present, and, indeed, the very concept of genre in still life can never be the same again. Nor can ever stop changing.

Thus the genre of still life undergoes a series of poetic revisions, in the light of its own history. From Cézanne to Morandi, both in his early "metaphysical" paintings and in his richly painted later ones (for which he often painted on the surfaces of his objects before setting them up to render them even more abstract or made up) to Bailey, who moves beyond his precursor in not setting up his arrays of kitchenware at all, but by assembling the collection of fictive objects on the canvas itself, the concept of still life is troped, made less literal, even further. That concept is as fruitful and elusive a one for Western painting as are comedy, or romance or even, in its complex way, sonnet (and are these genres, modes, forms?) for literature. The very fact of their history is the material out of which their novelty is shaped.

In Meyer Schapiro's splendid modern iconographic investigation of Cézanne's apples, he remarks on the modulation of prior *nature morte* into erotic offering. Rejecting the formalist view of the still life set-up as the optimum occasion for a painter's "concentrating on the problem of form" (he quotes Venturi's words here), Schapiro implicitly denies that the history of the genre, in which it gradually became laundered of emblem, mythology and even tokens of painterly skill (as, for example, in the case of Sébastien Stosskopff's 18th-century obsession with the setting up and painting of structures of wineglasses) must stop there. This formalistic view is, in its way, almost as narrowed as the grossly literal one, invoked by the literary critic Edmund Gosse, in 1898, in which he compares certain kinds of description in novels to "passages of an inventory or a still life" — as if inventories, lists, catalogues, blazons, parades from Homer to Whitman could not be poetical, nor still lifes anything but all-but-literal. Schapiro's own reading of Cézanne's complex refiguration of the human form by the canonical, textual (from Virgil's eclogues) fruit, psychoanalytic as it is, seems as challenging to any notions of "mere" formalism as that very dogma of modernity is to the concerns of the anecdotal, the moralizing, the trivially biographical.

* * *

What this comes down to is, among other things, the fact that all aesthetically responsible still life pictures of late modernity must not only show, but tell, in their own way. They not only invent and deploy their own visual languages, but they make their own kinds of statements about their relation, as images, to the rest of our world. Bailey's pursuit of his artistic quest through the wilderness of wildernesses, of deserts, jungles, pitfalls, quicksands, the "Rocks, caves, bogs, fens, lakes, dens, and shades of death" comprised by the bewilderments of possibility for painting in America since 1960, led him to an initial purity, in his first rather formalistically conceived paintings of eggs. In moving further onward, that purity never became corrupted by the temptations of the fussy, falsifying complexity to which thoughtful painters are sometimes prone. (There was little danger that he would slide into the swamps of sleazy sensationalism, pseudo - irony, or even the more trivial minimalism which has drawn back in such fear of other agendas that it almost vanishes into itself.) Bailey's purity outgrew its innocence but never broke faith with its point of departure — what John Ashbery has called "the mooring of starting out, that day so long ago" — and gained in strength.

He would also discover the kinds of utterance that his developing pictorial vocabulary could frame: Does this teapot preside over the group of eggs and cups around and about it, for instance? Or does it attend upon one or more of them like a large, looming servant? Have the objects on the left been abandoned to the claims of shadow, like a huddle of valley houses toward sundown? Or, on the other hand, are they emerging into a kind of epistemological, rather merely optical focus, a focus of attentive notice rather than of delineation? Is this group an instance of a scatter, a sprawl, a pile, a jumble, a bridge, a house, a ruin, a parade, a store, a frieze, a bunch, a gang, a mob, of elements? Are they somehow sacred, even though perhaps officially (that is, with respect to institutionalized sanctities) profane? What metaphoric version of practice, rite or ironic adoration do they command?

One obvious point is that each of his paintings, whether viewed individually or in a sort of serial light, poses its own kind of question. An earlier still life artist might construct a set-up to pose certain problems of drawing or of catching light, or of credibly rendering texture of some object's surface; the viewer then notices the difficulty overcome and applauds the skill. For Bailey's paintings we must acknowledge the metaphoric suggestions made, the relations revealed, and, increasingly in the past decade, the peculiar meditative tone, the particular cast of the atmosphere.

Some of this is a matter of Bailey's tonality and its particular meditative cast, the kind of twilight in which his objects and spaces are set. It is useful in this regard to consider some of his still life drawings and lithographs, in which, hue being excluded, tone must perforce play a very different part. In the 1988 *Via della Penna,* for instance, the particular tabled scene, read as if through an attenuating mist, keeps the entire range of tonal contrast to a minimum, the more perhaps to promote its local moments — the lip of the bowl on the viewers's left and of the pot, second right, and, largely because of the small scale of the enclosure, the oval space of the cup handle. (This drawing might be compared with the 1987 *Still Life,* with its greater tonal range.) On the other hand, the cast shadows are all of one hue with those that model and, indeed, with the objects which cast them: the interplay between those two sorts of shadow, so crucial to the structure of the paintings, is almost entirely suspended. One has only to compare the treatment of the tallest (fifth from the left) pot with that of a similar object in the *Via Alberti.*

It is also a matter of light. The light is non-literal, which is to say that the sources in each of the paintings do not derive from the sources in the studio, but are ad hoc

7. *Via della Penna,* 1988

8. *Still life,* 1987

to the painting in a way that helps to establish the nature of its fictive space. It is not ad hoc to a particular object, which might constitute a form of melodramatic or sentimental spotlighting. (It might be usefully compared, for example, with the way in which Walter Murch lit the surfaces of the brass clockwork and related objects to which the nostalgia in his painting was so devoted. There, the dusty highlighting is as of objects in a notional sort of museum-case, and the light and tone speak to a nostalgia for the function these objects once had, and the evanescent beauty they have when taken out of one literal context for another). But none of this is true of Bailey's paintings. They generate their own light, appropriately enlisting the illuminating power of each object: many of them glow, although in no way that could be associated with surface glitter. Mark Strand observed that "only the shadows cast on the background wall indicate an interior, but an interior that is paradoxically limitless." There is also a mutual generation of light and room in the spaces of his still life paintings; like Chardin's niches or kitchen tables, Bailey's visionary places are sacred (which is to say, set aside from ordinariness, imaginatively secluded), yet neither grossly supernatural nor crudely unremarkable. Andrew Forge has written of Bailey's light as only a painter (as well as only a writer) can:

"Light falls calmly on these objects, turning them slowly towards their greatest volume. It is a strong light, but spread, as through ground glass. It obeys rules of its own. Forms are modelled by it as though light was pressing flatly against the plane of the picture. But then there are shadows telling me that the light is coming from the right.

26

Nor do these shadows behave consistently. Sometimes they fall on curved surface as if it was flat. Sometimes they fall on the wall behind an object as though that wall was inches closer than it could possibly be. Sometimes they fall on objects as though those objects were seen at a great distance, in parallel vision, even though their surfaces are densely modelled... Light exerts a mysterious force, compressing and stretching space so that the still objects seem to hold their places in humming tension''.

The matter of shadow in Bailey's still lifes is a fascinating one, reminding us of some of the complexities of our very word "shadow," which itself has been used in English to mean "picture," "image," any kind of visual representation (as opposed to the "substance" which it represents), an element in allegorical typology, some kind of spiritual emanation of a person, even a verbal metaphor. Cast shadows are in a way figures of things, but in a realm even of partial visual abstraction they are things in themselves, of one painted substance, as it were, with their father objects. In this they are typical of representation in art, claiming as much authenticity for themselves as independent entities as for themselves as signifiers of more solid presences. In Bailey's world, objects cast shadows on that back wall, on the surface on which they stand, on other objects and, of course, on parts of themselves. This last is the familiar matter of modeling, of using occluded light to give metaphoric, two-dimensional shape to solid objects, the shading that the Greeks called *skiagraphia* or "shadow-drawing." But since Bailey's shadows are not usually employed for indicating caverns and holes — particularly in the paintings from about 1973 on — we must wonder what other functions they serve in what other sorts of substitute for narrative that make up a modern painting's story. Other than telling tales about mass and solidity and weight and texture in the poetic language of painted surface, what are shadows for?

In a painted realm for which tone is as significant as hue, concern for the matter of shadow and substance becomes heightened, and one must consider in reading any one of these compositions the relative significance of direct and of shadowed occlusion of an object by another one. Any painting will provide instances of this; almost at random, for example, we might consider the 1977 *Large Orvieto Still Life* for the way in which the small, white, flowered, covered pot (a sugar caster or salt shaker) encroaches upon the surface of the tall coffee-pot behind it: its own top and even its slanting left side cooperate far more genially with the painted form of the pot and its spout than does the incursive form of the shadow it casts upon its lower portion. At the same time, the more muted shadow of the handle of the adjacent brown pot just to the viewer's left of it is almost considerately contained within the form of the visible handle.

Indeed, what object casts what kind of shadow-form on what substance-form of what other nearby object can be in general a kind of commentary on the particular relation of adjacent objects in the set up. These secondary relations — of shadow-form to primary relations of substance form (including those often prominent, often recessive, forms created by the partial occlusions of objects by other ones) — become important elements of the "subject matter" in any particular painting. The "subject" of this uniquely conceived kind of still life is made of these relations and their parables — abstract in one sense, humanely concrete in another — of the many modes of contiguity; the fertile rhetoric with which painted objects make claims on available space for prominence or authority; the promotion of one detail over another as a badge of eminence or subordination; the nobility of size, the servility of bulk; the significance of the ways in which they and/or their shadows touch each other. And always

> The shadows that these pots cast on the bright
> Surfaces of adjacent ones make light
> Of weight, and darken only that they may
> Pretend to depth with all their weightless might.

But all this emerges only gradually in the course of Bailey's work. In an earlier painting such as the *Still Life with Eggs, Bowl and Vase* of 1971, the two ceramic objects are still surrounded by the primary eggs, and even, in the case of the bowl, containing them (an extremely rare visual event in these paintings). The tonal relations among the eggs, the geometric structures, exhibited by the front of the chest with its right hand door very slightly ajar, that occupy most of the lower half of the painting, and particularly the placing of the chest's top below eye level, cease to be prominent matters only a few years later. It is during the early seventies that some of the most familiar elements of the still life paintings begin to emerge, and to be explored.

In the first place there is the variety of the objects themselves, exhibiting a far greater range of form and color than previously. The anonymity of any particular egg surrenders to the recognizable presences of individual objects which reappear in different situations in successive canvases. Pots, as we know, can achieve transmuted glory. It is not that this cup is Sèvres, that jug blue-hoop from Woolworth's, with rank and title taking precedence as in a kingdom or a shop-window. It is rather how, in any moment of assembly, these painted fictions can engender new orders and values. The refined china cup, green-edged, enters one of these paintings as a frail object, while the homely, blue-banded bowl can exhibit almost regal munificence and generosity. We may muse on the three-dimensional ancestors of these objects, the crockery gathering contemplative dust in Bailey's studio, abstracted from their literal qualities of surface in the light of his paint. (Although he never looks at the objects while painting

10. *Nogna,* 1986

11. *Manhattan still life,* 1980

— and certainly never arranges them in a set-up, a version of each inhabitant of the paintings exists, whether in a random grouping on the studio shelf or, in the painter's own words, "on the other side of the ocean." It is as if, in order to participate in the ceremonies of art, in their rebirth as images, they had to leave their surfaces — their roughness or sheen, their rumors of porosity and reflectiveness — behind at the door of the painted world, to re-emerge in a realm of tone. And once there, their frontality is sometimes of an ancestral or commemorative photograph, but of a family group, never a football team.

There is the matter, too, of gestural signification in the forms of more complex objects. Consider the *Mercatale Still Life,* an autumnal picture, a group of structures in a late light: the sad, almost noble attenuation of what on the studio shelf was a wooden potato-masher makes for its own sort of verticality. (And how much more attenuated it seems in the later *Nogna,* where the vertical of the angle in the wall affects it so strongly). The china cup mentioned above plays a particular role here. Else-

12. *Still life Umbertide,* 1981

where, as in the *Monterchi Still Life,* pointing out with its handle towards the viewer's left, it lends no part to the official configuration of the other objects, seemingly turning away from them. Here, it plays the role not of a refuser to align, but of a guardian of the margin in that flatter array of objects which seem to be regarding the light source, bidding it a kind of shipboard farewell. (But consider its different role, in a similar position, in the *Manhattan Still Life* of a year earlier.)

On the other hand, tonal affinity may become a central issue in a particular painting, as in *Umbertide.* The declarations of blue and white give importance to the lighter strip (of partially rotated white panel) on the edge of the vase on the left, mediating the contiguity of the same vase's cast shadow: it is as if that strip were not merely the leftward limit of the array (at that height), but an ambiguous region between shadow and substance, as if overlapping mind and body in a philosophical problem.

By 1973, Bailey's table-tops, whether extending horizontally to the edge of the painting or contained, as finite objects, within its space, had begun to be fixed at eye-level. It was never that his pots (with the rare exception noted above) were to be thought of as full or empty: this matter is not part of their being, nor does it enter their metaphoric life, and if they are to be thought of as containers, then they might only be said to be full of their own surfaces. But it is finally when the objects are all at eye level, or almost so, that the issue of modeling or rounding has to be in-

13. *Migianella still life with tureen,*
   1973

dependent of any possible empty space inside them — it is as if they were all unhollowed solids. It is also finally at this time that a particularly architechtonic — even an almost architectural — quality of the compositions begins to emerge. More and more the groups of objects look not so much to lie in prospect on a plain (they are often palpably and pointedly shelved or tabled), but to stand in an outdoor light, occluding a horizon rather than merely a back wall.

Interestingly, too, this is about the time when his titles begin to reflect, very faintly and figuratively, the association of still life compositions with particular places, most often in Italy, and always beloved. In 1972 Bailey and his wife Sandra, bought a house in Umbria, on land near a ruined castle called Migianella dei Marchesi, which name started showing up in the titles of works completed or started there (e.g. *Migianella Still Life with Tureen*). These place-name-titles have remained; the association is varyingly direct or oblique, and sometimes, Bailey avers, unwitting; yet they always seem now more appropriate to the objects arrayed as much like elevations of architectural structures as like groups of persons than, say, *Still Life 5, 1986* or *Still Life Against Green Back Wall* would be. But in any case they are never in any way literal (so that, for example, one should not look among the objects in the *Deruta Still Life* for a cup or bowl of characteristic painted pottery named for that city of its manufacture).

In the more recent paintings the space becomes more complicated, and the architectural implications show up in another way. Bends and angles, sometimes doubled as if around a vertical beam, start to occur in the wall behind, for example, seeming to reflect an impulse to change the earlier pattern in which a large scale element — the wall behind — was inactive (in the sense of being devoid of incident), and all activity (incident) confined to the smaller range of scale. (But, of course, never at the

a

b

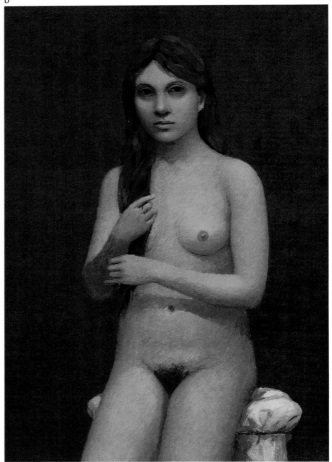

smallest level of scale, which would constitute fussy detail.) In the paintings of the past decade, having an angle in the wall acknowledges that an incident can indeed occur at the largest scalar level. The interior space as well as the vertical plane start to become articulated with the introduction of the vertical jumps in the walls and their cast shadows, not to speak of domelike, very shallow niches in paintings like *Bettona* of 1988. In all these, the architectural quality is all the more confirmed.

Both the wall angle and the vertical format which we see more and more in the most recent work stem from "The Hexagonal Room," a project in 1981 on which he worked with the architect Cesar Pelli for the Architectural League of New York, and for which Bailey did two still lifes and a nude in casein on panel. They were placed around a hexagonal table inside a small hexagonal building, in such a way that opposite each painting one finds the table, a chair and, behind the chair, a window. What might look at first glance like a sort of gazebo or summer-house, is in fact a sanctuary for contemplation, not only of the paintings but of the nature of the sanctuary provided by the building, and of the relations between these. Bailey himself recalls that "the verticals of the framing structure seemed to call for a major vertical response in the paintings," which response involved the introduction of angled wall, at first only as a sort of vertical strip, later with additional complexities.

The introduction of the interior corner raised, from the very first, interesting questions for the metaphoric relations of the composed objects. One might compare the *Via Alberti* painting with the *Piazza Fortebraccio,* brown, soft-edged, its tonality making the role of its white forms less a hierarchic or even a political matter, the whole composition claiming sovereignty over the corner on the left by clustering its objects there. In *Via Alberti,* the whites and blues are somehow elite, and the tall vase on the left and the candlestick next to it occupy what is clearly their corner. These corners generate

14. *Hexagonal room,* 1981
   a) still life
   b) figure
   c) still life

their rooms' interiors in no anecdotal sense. Rather, a new formal element has lent another layer of possible meanings to the implications of gathering studied in earlier paintings, where objects huddle, range, couple or protect, attend upon, assist, face up to, and even upstage one another. Spatial constructions grew to include such matters as that of the strip-hung shelf in the 1988 *Borgo,* which seems to make an almost witty comment or some of the developing spatial complexities of the previous years.

Bailey paints still life, then, as if all set-ups, however "abstract" or "structural" (like some of Morandi's preserved in photographs), were far too narrative, however implicitly — far too fictional in a literary way rather than fictive or abstract in a pictorial one. For there are residues of story lurking in the set-up itself, the traces of an activity — not of crudely *using* the objects, of drinking from them, or pouring from or into them — but of more subtly employing them in the life of the studio. His objects are thus neither at work nor at trivial play — standing upside-down, say, or piled into precarious constructions, or enchanted into disorientations of scale or grounding, as by Magritte. Even these compositions might be deemed too anecdotal. One of Bailey's ways of transcending the almost sectarian realms of the "real," the "poetic," the "sentimental," the "narrative" is through this kind of distancing in design and execution, and in some strange way this corresponds with the kinds of distance — visual, epistemological, personal — separating the viewer from his table-tops, and even from his posed models.

15. *Borgo,* 1988

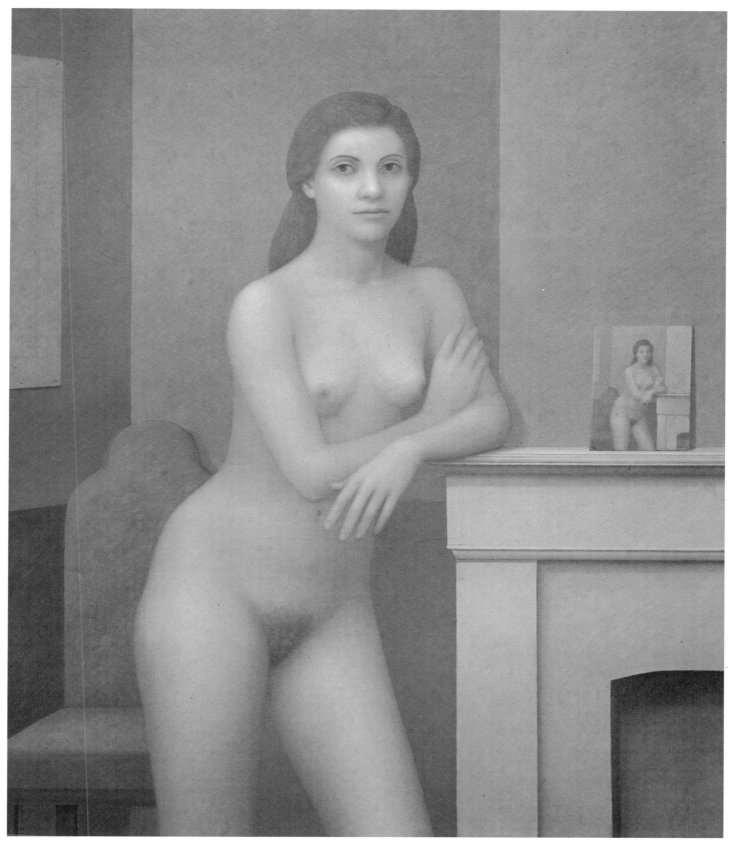

16. «*K*», 1986-88

His objects thus inhabit a world free of literal memories and desires, devoid of *souvenirs* although not of *mémoire,* and unencumbered by appeals to the passions of the eye which empower *trompe-l'oeil,* or to those passions of imagined touch to which loaded brushwork and luscious painterly devotion to objects' surfaces variously appeal. The finest moments in this world are of meditative rest, and the mental use of the objects is in an iconography of relations far more abstract than would occur in punning resemblances or in a surrealistic rebus. Visible painted evidence of such relations emerges from these objects in a certain kind of repose, even as modern urban landscape can become poetic when wiped bare of the easy irony which is so like sentimentality.

* * *

The relation of Bailey's figure paintings to his still lifes is a fascinating one. They both involve an abstraction from previous generic fictions. In view of the contracted mythology and absence of narrative in Bailey's figure-paintings, we might observe at the outset how *K,* worked on from 1986 to 1988, raises some relevant questions. The image, called in the language of heraldry, *en abîme* — the smaller panel on the mantelpiece almost replicating the entire painting — is not a literary device. In view of the unnecessary celebration of self-referentiality in recent discourse about literature and art, perhaps it is well to point this out at once. Muddle-headed confusions between any kind of allusiveness, internal or external to the work, and what is inanely called irony, are often made by painters totally unaware of what the term usefully means. It should therefore be made plain, I think, that the reduplication of the image here is unclouded by any trace of uneasy denigrative joking about what representation is: Bailey almost insists on this by erasing the image of the image of the image from what is seen in the mantelpiece picture. The pictured model-in-her-place, tilted very slightly forward, inhabits a far more flattened domain than the one in her panel does; and even though its overall rectangle is very slightly narrower, the contained image is like a planar map of the primary one.

By preventing the infinite regress, and the literary trickery that might accompany it, the painter nonetheless contracts for a certain amount of narrative speculation. It is not that the significance of K's frontal look becomes more of a personal gaze: her eyes, as always, are points of tonal extreme, rather than dark flashlights of attentive scrutiny, or unshuttered but curtained windows out of which the soul is not looking at the moment, but rather scrutinizing its souvenirs. Yet two possible traces of story flicker across this painting: the painter has done a previous smaller painting of the identical pose, on a panel, which he now sets up on the mantelpiece and includes in the larger painting. This would, of course, have to be a fiction generated by the painting itself, given what we know of the artists's rigorously abstract practice. The picture of herself, hung not on the wall behind her as in some Dutch painting as an emblematic commentary on the scene before it, nor as a piece of authentic furniture in a documentary interior, depicts the model's thought of herself. That thought is not of an erotic object for painter or viewer. Nor is it of a heroic personage — that Goddess of the Studio who, in modern art, stands in as lovingly paintable body for the narrative figures of Christian Scripture, history or classical myth. It is rather of the model as model, as a person who surrenders some of what can be seen of her to what will be made of her in paint. And this is why the second-order of image-within-the-image is not there: it would be totally absent from her thought. Bailey's painting does not demand that we settle for either of these stories. But the relation between the abstractedness of the model's relation to her image here, and the purely notional (as always) set-up, is an interesting one and a kind of little parable in itself.

This painting can also be considered as a version of the *Portrait of MDH* of the same year, in which the figure is posed almost — but not quite — identically, with respect to a white, untapered, fluted cup. As early as the 1970 *Sisters,* with the vase

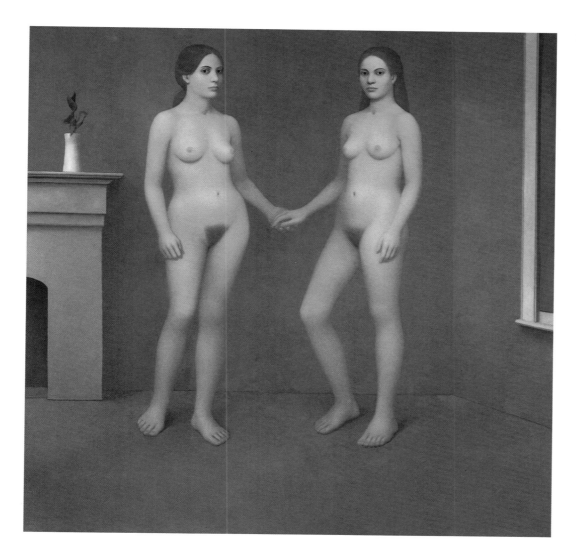

of flowers on its mantelpiece to the left, Bailey had composed relations between nudes and objects, but the painting of *L* (1986) seems also to recapitulate some of the issues implicit in the largely unstated, but continuously developing, relation between the nude and the still life pictures. Here the ''story'' is one of the relation of the nude figure and the familiar cup. But in *L,* that graceful handle which is ever-present in various rotations in the still-lifes of the previous decade, as well as occupying the same end of a mantelpiece in various figure paintings at least as early as the 1978 *Agostina,* is totally occluded. Its sombre tonality recalls that of the very early (1963) *Girl in Green Room,* in which, however, the walls and ceiling, which occupy most of the painting, are the subject of considerable painterly attention, and the figure seems to be emerging out of a world governed by an abstract agenda suggested by the flattening of the depth of room in the upper-right-center, and in which she is still — at this point in Bailey's work — almost, in another sense of the word, cornered. She is also directly lit; and it is almost as if she were only beginning to emerge from a previous figural existence, to enter a new kind of space, and a world lit as no corner of any studio ever has been. (Like the early ''pre-still life'' *Untitled,* this painting has a touch of the quiet manifesto about it.)

That emergence is almost, but not quite, complete in the painting of *N* in 1964. Its title designates both the model (''Nan'') and for the ''N''-shaped form suggested by the conformation of head and trunk, thigh, and lower leg, as if ''N'' were a sort of conceptual armature for the figure. The model is still exemplifying the structure, and her image is as much of that structural element as it is of her: in this, the double denotation of the title of the painting is almost a generic statement. There is a mute dialogue between the prominent form — almost like that of a piece of pottery — of her right hip and buttock (explored again in a much later drawing of 1981 and those in the sequence of blue, white and olive pillows behind her. In Bailey's later figures, a positional paradigm will play a different sort of role. The one for the figure in *K* and *MDH* seems to come from a drawing of Ingres, a study for his portrait of the Princesse de Broglie of 1853, and the very nature of its faint allusiveness is more a matter of a kind of secret spell for the painter himself than of a schema or a sign. It could be observed that Ingres' great importance for Bailey shows both more palpably and more profoundly in his still life than in his figure paintings, although there are memories of Ingres' *odalisques* present in the 1963 *Seated Nude with Clasped Hands*.

A theorist of the nature of modeling has said that the artist's *model* ceases to exist as such when the person doing the posing dresses, or gets out of costume, and leaves: he or she becomes merely a person again. And so of the object: ''Natalie's cup'' (in the casein on paper *Still Life with Natalie's Cup* becomes a model for a while,

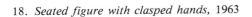

18. *Seated figure with clasped hands,* 1963

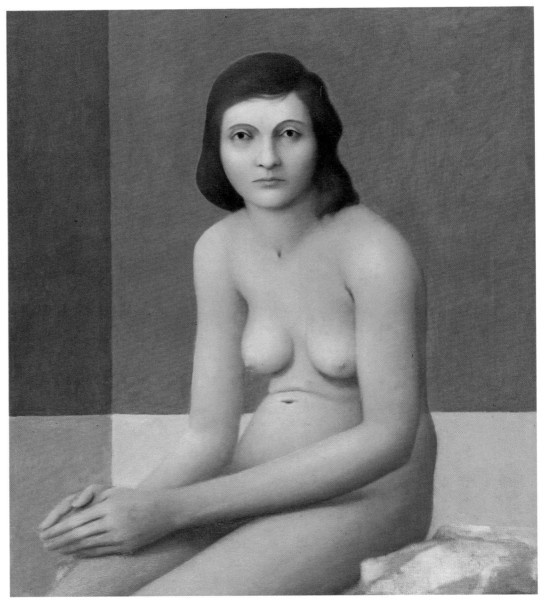

38

and then may be returned to Natalie to drink out of. But in neither case will the personhood of the model, nor the useful objecthood of the cup be the subject of representation in Bailey's art. They are only there as the painter has cast them in the particular roles that they play in the particular visual theater of a particular painting. This question of the variety of similar roles of narrative or emblem played by the model and the object (as excluded by Bailey's kind of painting) reminds one of how persons and things may, in the cinematic sense, work as stand-ins for one another. The theoretical writer Louis Marin has suggested that the history of still life considered with respect to the bourgeois preference for middle-class interiors instead of heroic scenes was nevertheless accompanied by some structural questions of composition that remain constant between them. In this instance it should be added that objects can become surrogates for persons, even as the lusciously non-empty table-top in the middle-class room can become a metaphorical version of — rather than a simple, unconnected replacement for — the scene wherein heroic narrative, whether biblical, historical or mythological, takes place.

The evolving concerns in Bailey's paintings of female figures — never male ones — have led him to cast them in a variety of roles. Of the paintings of the late 1970s, Mark Strand has observed that "while the still lifes have gained in complexity, the figures have become more simple. No longer the tableaux of a cultivated and rehearsed intimacy, nor the ironic projections of a ceremonial nakedness, nor meditations on posing reminiscent of Balthus, Bailey's figures have eased off into a naturalness that suggests certain figures of Corot." We may trace some of this through a sequence of nudes over the years.

The placing and spacing of the three figures in the very early *Stage* of 1964 respond to the most abstract of agendas: the three figures' respective relations to bed, mantelpiece and chair, and those relations' more general role in the play of rectangles within the painting, nullify the narrative question that any group of three figures will

39

usually raise. We do not wonder whether these figures are projections of the same person, whether they represent three modes or conditions of waiting, or whether perhaps they are three sisters (and thus, possibly, dark Graces, young Fates, etc.); their systematically averted gazes (from the others, from the viewer, from anything) are simply not at issue. While something like a motif that we might call "The Model and the Mantel" does indeed seem, in the light of the later nudes, to emerge from the center of this group, the figures themselves speak a sequence of different silent languages.

The figure in *French Room,* worked on from 1965—67, is closely related to the central one in *Stage.* Yet she inhabits what is clearly a visionary room. It will become in later figure paintings a kind of mythical chamber, derived from observed studio space, remembered interior spaces. This enclosure lingers in a kind of light — here, still plausibly coming from the window on the left (which reveals only its framing moldings as vertical analogues of the horizontals of the mantelpiece) — which both the figure paintings and still lifes would eventually forego. She is schematically posed with respect to the rectangle of the (viewer's) left side of the fireplace, her right forefinger just touching the line of its edge.

These relations of the pose of the figure to the geometrical forms generated by elements of room interior and furniture become more subtle in later paintings. In *Perugina* the prominent angularity of the half-lozenge of draped cloth speaks in oblique ways of the square generated by the balletic rotation of the figure's back leg, of the angularity across the vertical fall of hair made by the right forearm, and even of dissimilar triangle of the void between her left arm and side. In *L* of 1986, the matter of such relations becomes still more complex in the very range, from direct to oblique, of the relations of the more "geometrically" posed figure to the horizontals and verticals of the objects which she touches, and the structures of the spaces she and they inhabit.

In the partly clothed 1978 figure of *Agostina,* the geometric issue became even more intricate and, ultimately, involved with matters of representation at another level. Table, chair and mantel crowd and virtually exhaust the horizontal space across the painting — in particular, the rectangle created by the angle of the walls is completely filled — as well as half the depth within it. But there is the additional complications of the figure's cast shadow, far more abstract than *vero,* falling on the wall and faintly avoiding the cup. Unusual in these figure paintings, the shadow seems to involve the hand-held mirror in a strange way. The model is no more contemplating herself in what resembles an antique Roman bronze mirror than, indeed, either she or the shadow are drinking from the cup. It is the entirety of Bailey's picture which leads her to hold it, and not any narrative determinant — "Agostina" is not Venus, nor Vanitas, nor Prudence; she is not an Umbrian or New England girl caught by some visionary camera in a moment of blank reflection as she turns her gaze away from the reflection of herself; she is not the model dutifully holding up some prop to provide either a needed position of arm and hand, or a needed bit of visual event to inhabit the largest area of uninterrupted space in the painting. But it *is* a mirror, even if unreflecting and unconsulted; and, as if in some kind of acknowledgment of this, the figure's ambiguously cast shadow stands in, to our gaze, for a mirrored reflection. But it is the tonally marked angle, almost following one of the paintings main diagonals, and leading from the figure's left hand — at the center of the painting — up to her right one, and from which the mirror's axis deviates a bit, that helps to place the object in the particular world of the painting.

Agostina is one of a number of bare-breasted but skirted nudes that Bailey did between 1976 and 1980. They are all seated figures and it is as if the consequent skin folds above the belly, complicating the "form already purified" of the figure's body, seemed to call up an echoing complication below, in the rhyming line of the top of the petticoat, or, ambitiously, as in the *Girl in White Skirt,* where the opened top of the dress, and the V-shaped shadow it forms in her lap that seems about to fall into the cup of her right hand. Even more complex are the formal relations set up by the rolled-down dress and sleeves in the well-known *Portrait of S,* in which the various textures of curly hair and dress fabric threaten to disrupt the more usual relations between the quietude of surface and the non-referential kind of room. It is perhaps in response to this that the background plane behind the figure — no longer even the wall of a room, but an expanse of modern painted surface — is, for Bailey, unusually worked-up. But it was probably the distractions of drapery, of dealing with representations of fabric that seems to have a life of its own, that caused him to move away from the partially draped figure and return to the standing nude.

In all these cases, the light sources are as vagrant and ad hoc as in the still life pictures. This is even noticeable in the three paintings done for the "Hexagonal Room" project mentioned earlier: the actual illumination within the structure cast on the walls occupied by the three paintings (on the still lifes from the windows, on the nude from the oculus in the roof), is represented only allusively by the light in the paintings themselves. In general, the nude figures generate their own light, without ever glowing, in a way analogous to that by which Balthus' figures seem to secrete their own local surrounding spaces. And the light in Bailey's figure paintings is very different from that in the still lifes in most other ways.

The figures in the drawings are another matter, of course, and not only because they do not present figures in rooms or room-like spaces, in which the question of light falling on and around objects is at issue. More significantly, they are all the results of direct observation from the model, rather than set up on the canvas, like the still lifes, with at most an allusive relation to the drawn model. Noticeable too is the variety of these figures: their range of postures (with both structural and allusive consequences), their degrees of openness or closure, concentration on face or larger contour, and always, the prominence of the marks of drawing itself, and the prominence

21. *French room,* 1965-67

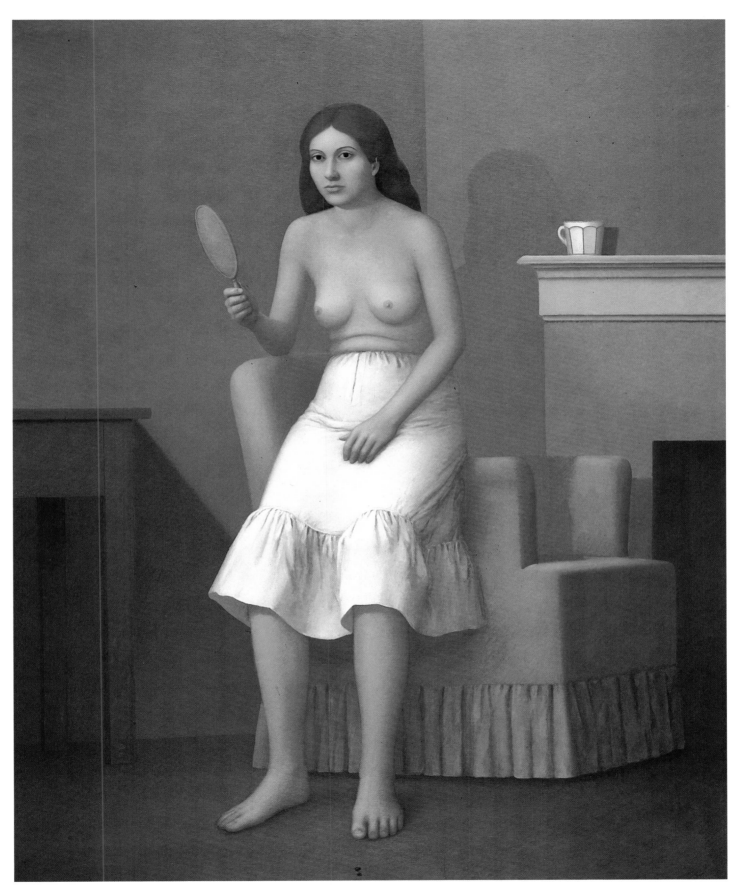

22. *Agostina,* 1978

of their role in modeling or implying volume. In the drawings, it is as if the models have had thoughts of Ingres or Balthus or Corot on their minds as they took up poses.

But if the spirit of Ingres helps shape the painted objects in the still life, it left only one simple message for the drawings, i.e. in regard to the relation of specificity and generalization. In many of these figure drawings, we do not get the literal clustering of detail in the face, and the trailing away to more ghostly suggestion in the fabric and body below. But the incompleted extremities — in particular, the feet whose minute particulars would provide a profound distraction to the apprehension of the tonality of the drawing — are by no means egregious. They take part in a larger and more abstract play of movement, not of modeled form, not of rhythm of line, but of the transitions of specificity and generality, which play like another order of light across the extent of the figures. In other instances, such as the *Reclining Figure* of 1981 the relation of darkest tone (the modeling shadow where the two calves cross) and areas of greatest detail (usually the face) is reversed; only the figure's left heel, having completed its work of breaking the curve made by the two soles and re-directing up toward the right buttock and hip, seems free to relax into generalization.

In any case, Bailey's drawings respond to direct observation by allowing the presence of the model to call up a system of marks, rather than a system of construction's seeming to generate the figures in their painted spaces. (Or even, indeed, the matter of medium in the paintings in casein on paper: there, another issue emerges with the texture of the paper's insisting on a faint rippling of painted line, a decreased luminosity, increased opacity, and a general flattening of space even as the texture of the picture plane becomes more momentarily active).

* * *

Abjuring the world of society in which combat, eros and law are constantly entangled, refusing to contest for crowns of oak, palm or laurel, the seventheenth-century poet Andrew Marvell's protagonist of "The Garden" retires to an enclosed world of a green which transcends the red and white of flesh and blood, of purity and passion. In it, no particular emblematic leaves single out particular realms of enterprise; rather "all flowers and all trees do close / To weave the garlands of repose." The world of William Bailey's painting seems to involve the weaving and the wearing of just such garlands — the task and the reward which, in art, are one. It is the place of retirement from one kind of engagement (with the aesthetic politics of representation, perhaps with the demoralized aftermath of abstract expressionism's assured vigor) into a world of active meditation.

But there is no loss here of sensuality or energy or those vigorous encounters with the problematic that differentiate true art from the mere manufacture of paintings: it is just that his pictures experience all these in their own terms. They might each be thought to occur in some kind of reinvented *hortus conclusus* or walled garden, a place of thoughtful delight, marked by promising — never menacing —shadows of what it had walled out. In the nude paintings, the place is always clearly a room inhabited by the figure, although the way in which she helps to generate the space around her makes for — as with all important figure painting — a new story of what it means to take up space, of what it means to be a figure *in* a place. We might call it a matter of each serious painter's giving a slightly different meaning to the preposition "in" — or at any rate, to the particular two-dimensional metonymy of three-dimensional spatial situations which characterize his or her particular painted worlds.

So, too, with the still lifes throughout the developement of Bailey's oeuvre, and the spaces they are *in,* the places they are *at,* the groups and structures they are *of,* all in their own unique senses of those prepositions. While never once specifically alluding to previous phases in the history of still life painting, those objects so arrayed among their own shadows, doing nothing but being there, seem peculiarly full of silent thought about the painted past. From the earliest classical stories of truth in paint-

ing, which devolved upon fables of *trompe-l'oeil,* through modernity's demands that an image be a credible part of its own painted domain, the Truth of Motionless Objects — as Ruskin might have termed it — emerges in Bailey's work as what I have previously called *trompe-l'apprehension.* It is an art not of illusion, but of the problems of impalpable fiction, of contemplative narratives in which tone, light, shadow and structural as well as formal innuendo contend for significance. Not the eye, but the understanding — of what these sets of objects and relations, in their places, in their spaces represent — is seduced, and the realization of what has happened unfolds more slowly than the mere shattering of illusion. It is an art that teases us out of thought and then deep into it again, and thereby becomes an art of the highest reality.

John Hollander

Woodbridge, Connecticut, May 1990

24. *Italian profile,* 1963

25. *Still life with ten eggs white vase,* 1971

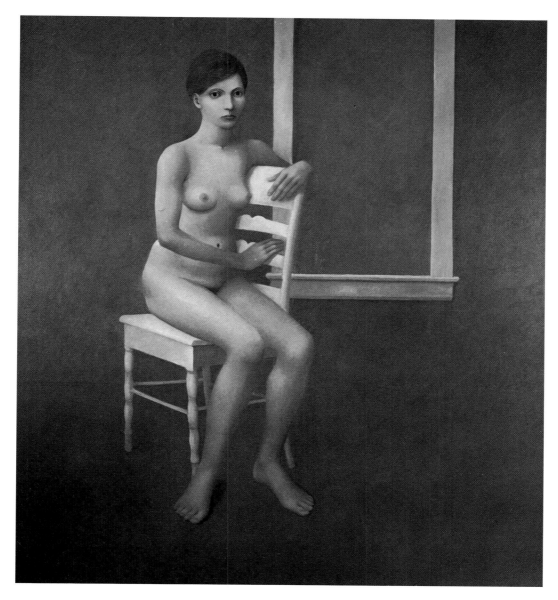

26. *Visitor,* 1963

27. *Still life with kitchen objects,* 1970

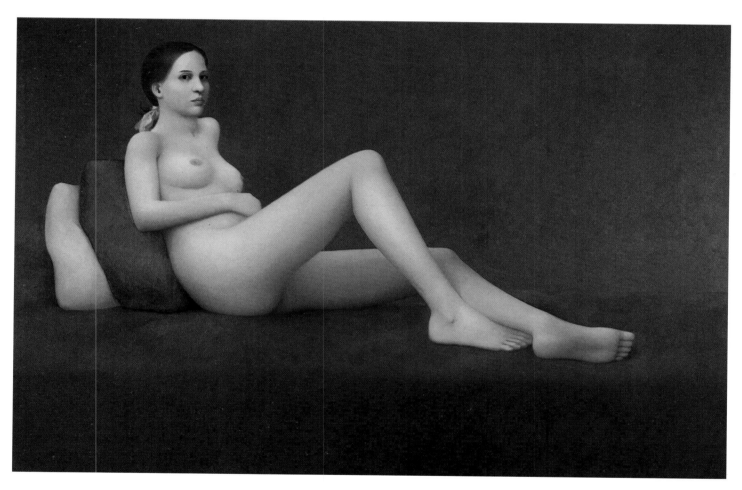

28. «*N*», 1964

29. *Eggs,* 1965

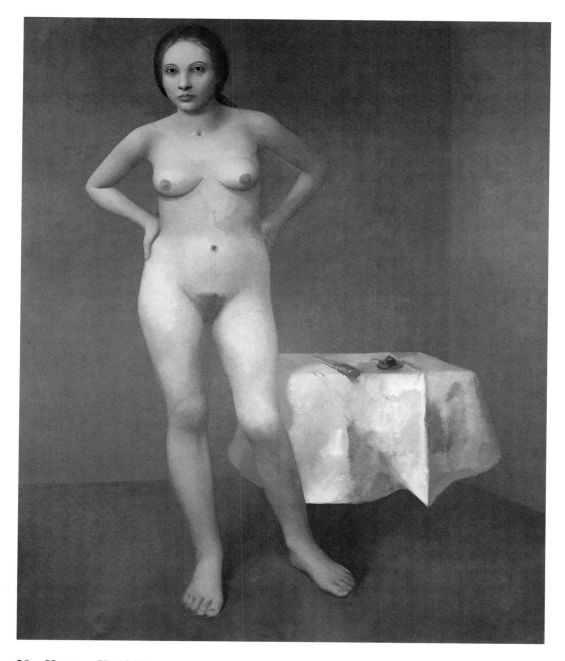

30. *Hostess II*, 1965

31. *Still life with egg cup, eggs and bowl, 1968-69*

32. *Still life with eight eggs,* 1970

33. *Portrait study,* 1970

34. *Still life with rose wall,* 1972

35. *Eggs, cup, cloth,* 1970

36. *Still life with eggs and blue-white bowl*, 1971

37. *Egg, cup and eggs,* 1970

38. *Eggs on mantelpiece,* 1970

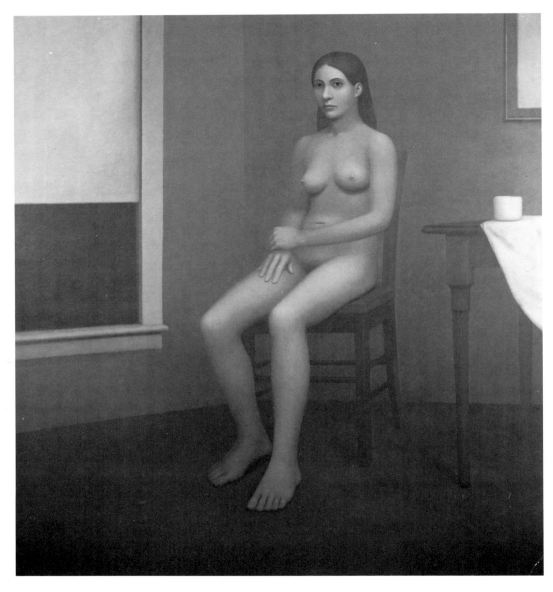

39. *Listener,* 1970-71

40. *Still life with eggs, bowl and vase,* 1971

41. *Still life with bowl, eggs,* 1976

42. *Still life Migianella with pitcher,* 1974

43. *Still life Montone,* 1977

44. *Still life Migianella,* 1976

45. *Migianella still life with eggs and coffee pot, 1975-76*

46. *Still life Roma,* 1976

47. *Small Orvieto still life,* 1977

48. *Girl in white skirt*, 1977

49. *Fratta,* 1978

50. *Still life with rose wall and compote*, 1977

51. *Grecian still life, 1978*

52. *Large Rome still life,* 1977

53. *Still life with red-brown wall,* 1978

54. *Still life Manfroni,* 1978

55. *Large umbrian still life,* 1978

56. *Piazza Fortebraccio,* 1981

57. *Still life Torre Gentile,* 1979

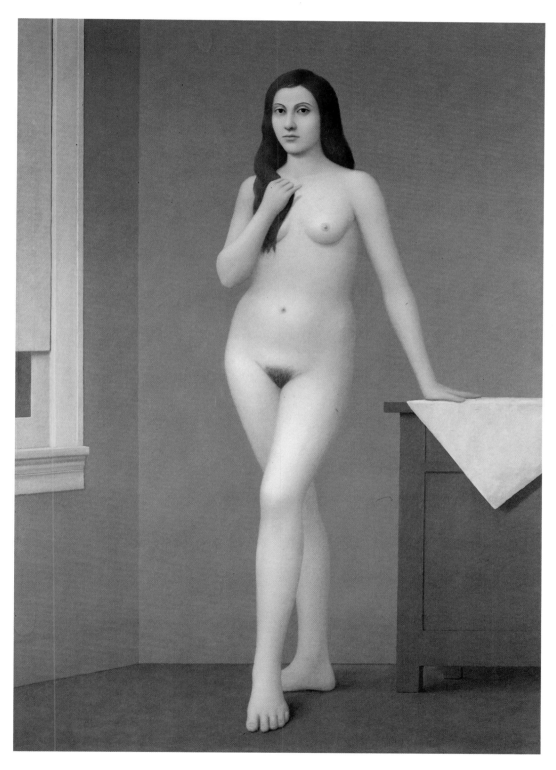

58. *Perugina,* 1982

59. *Still life Montefalco,* 1979

60. *Still life Monte Migiana*, 1980

61. *Still life Bevagna,* 1980

62. *Still life Castel Rigone,* 1980

63. *Still life Città di Castello,* 1980

64. *Study for visitor,* 1980

65. *Still life Monterchi,* 1981

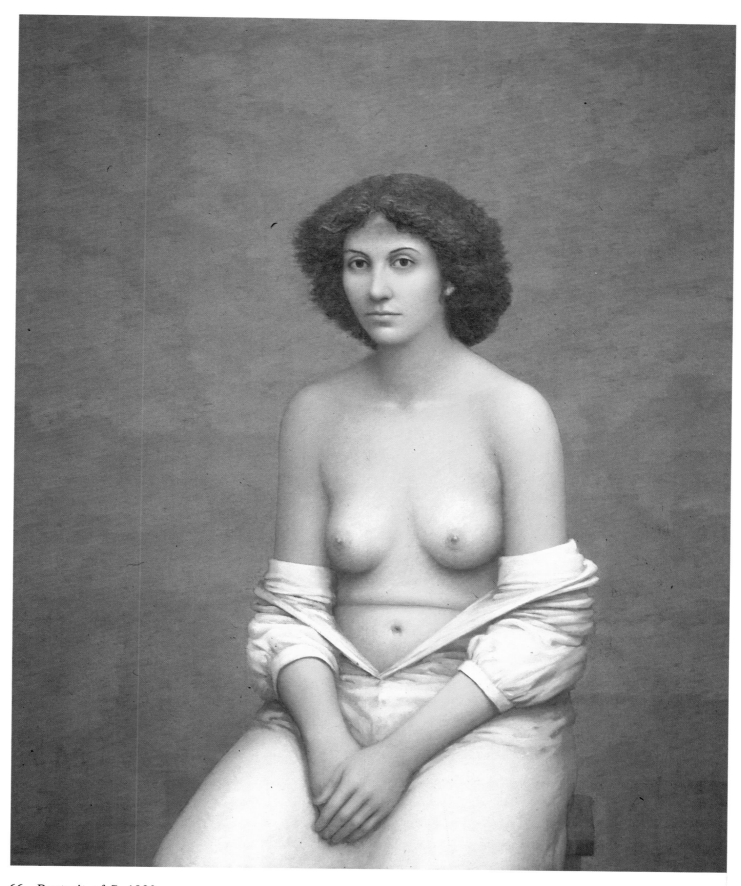

66. *Portrait of S,* 1980

67. *Still life Norcia,* 1982

68. *Still life Umbrian II*, 1982

69. *Still life Trevi,* 1982

70. *Still life Torre,* 1984

71. *Still life Trestina,* 1984

72. *Still life Genova,* 1984

73. *Still life Galera*, 1982

74. *Still life Pietralunga,* 1983

75. *Still life Villa Aurelia,* 1983

76. *Still life Calzolaro,* 1983

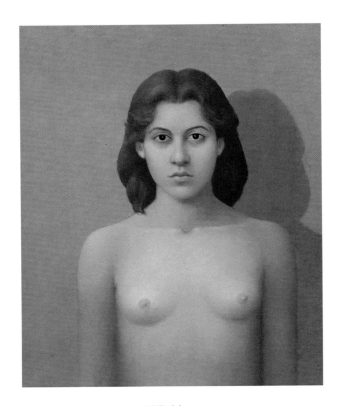

77. *Small figure,* 1977-83

78. *Still life Pisa,* 1984

79. *Still life Paestum,* 1985

80. *Still life Hotel Raphael,* 1985

81. *Still life Hotel Locarno,* 1985

82. *Still life Pierle,* 1987

83. *East rock,* 1987

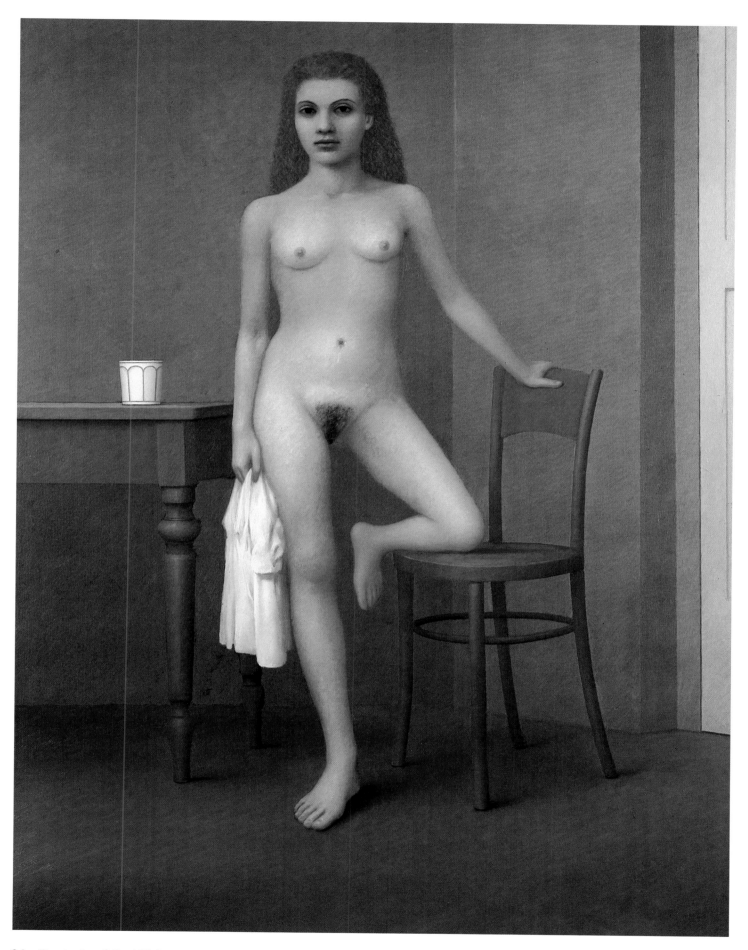

84. *Portrait of L*, 1986

85. *Still life Noto,* 1986

86. *Duomo,* 1987

87. *Study for visitor,* 1988

88. *Still life Civitella,* 1987

89. *Still life Bettona,* 1988

90. *Looking east,* 1988

91. *Still life Verona,* 1988

92. *Peck street,* 1989

93. *Paesaggio senese II,* 1989

94. *Montalcino,* 1989

95. *Still life Terontola,* 1988

96. *Mensola,* 1989

97. *Strada bianca,* 1990

120

98. *Pian del Voglio,* 1990

99. *Small still life,* 1978

100. *Ginepro,* 1978

101. *Ginepro,* 1978

102. *Ginepro n. 1,* 1979

103. *Ginepro n. 4,* 1980

104. *Ginepro n. 5,* 1980

105. *Ginepro n. 6,* 1980

106. *Deruta,* 1983

107. *Still life Piazza San Francesco,* 1982

108. *Pieroni,* 1981

109. *Montelovesco,* 1982

110. *Marsciano,* 1982

128

111. *Acquasparta,* 1987

112. *Castiglione,* 1983

113. *San Pancrazio,* 1984

114. *Study,* 1985

115. *San Liberato,* 1984

116. *Still life Preggio,* 1986

117. *Via Angelo Masina,* 1983

118. *Pergo,* 1987

134

119. *Still life Livorno,* 1987

120. *Paesaggio senese,* 1989

121. *Still life Montecastelli,* 1988

122. *Untitled,* 1990

123. *Girl dressing*, 1961

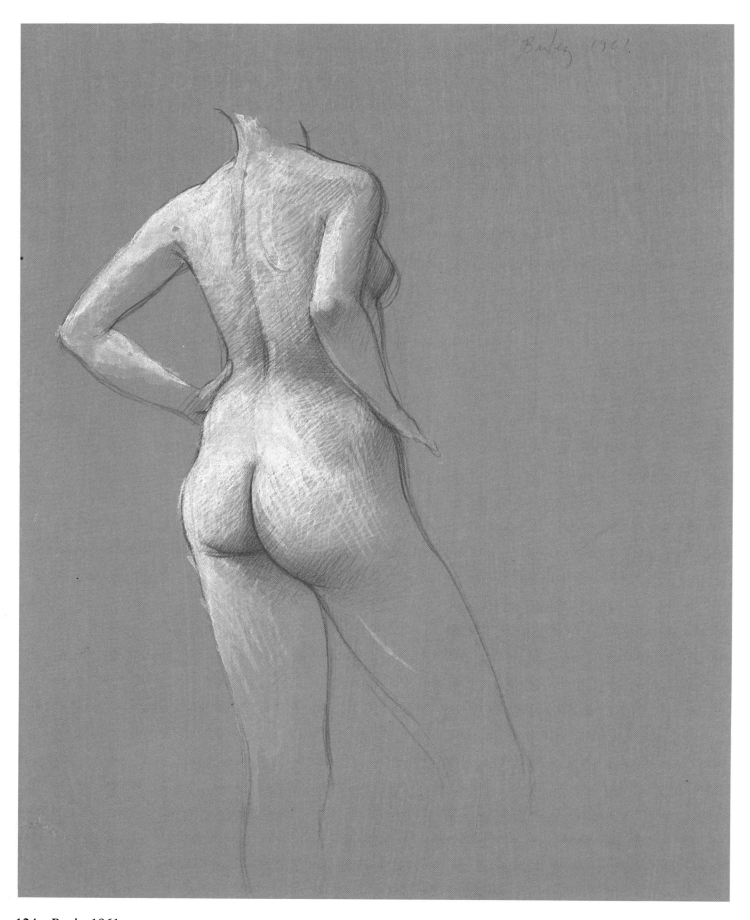

124. *Back,* 1961

125. *Portrait,* 1961

126. *Figure,* 1984

127. *Figure,* 1984

128. *Head,* 1984

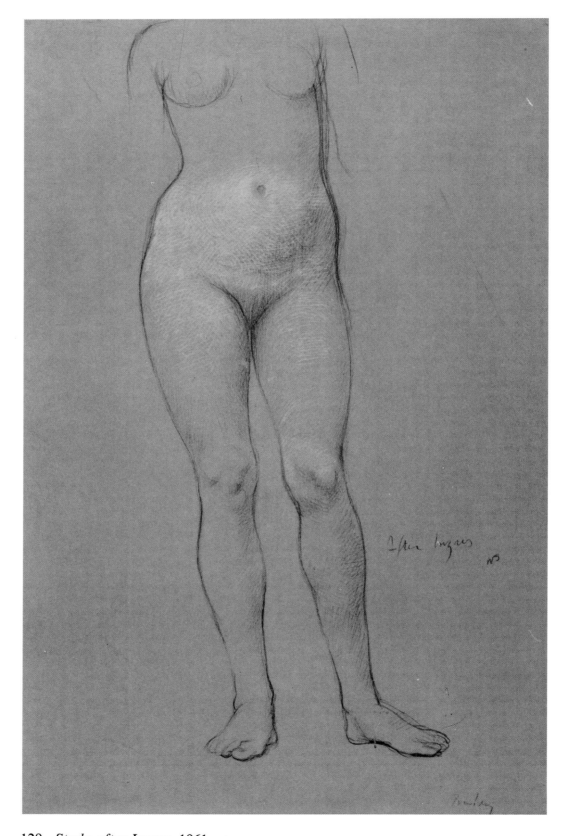

129. *Study after Ingres,* 1961

130. *Head,* 1961

131. *Seated figure,* 1970

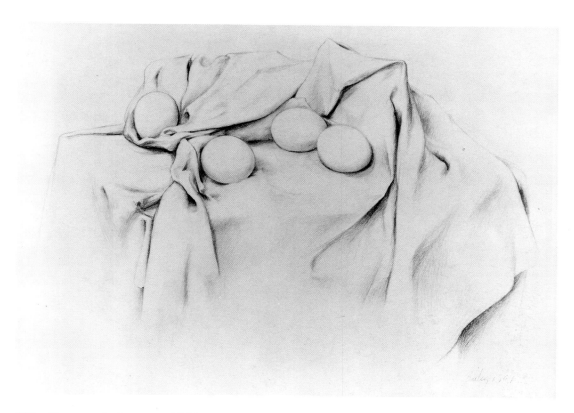

132. *Eggs and drapery,* 1961

133. *Seated figure,* 1974

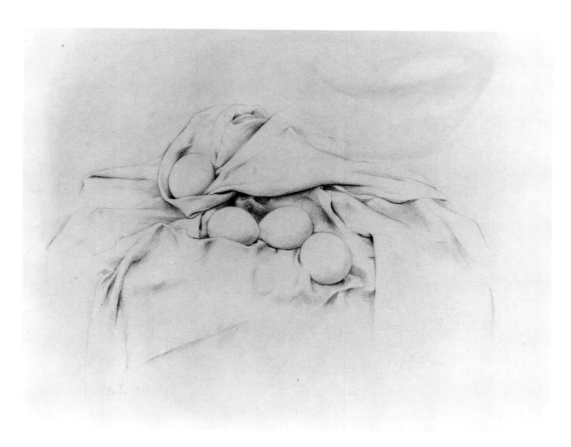

134. *Eggs and drapery,* 1961

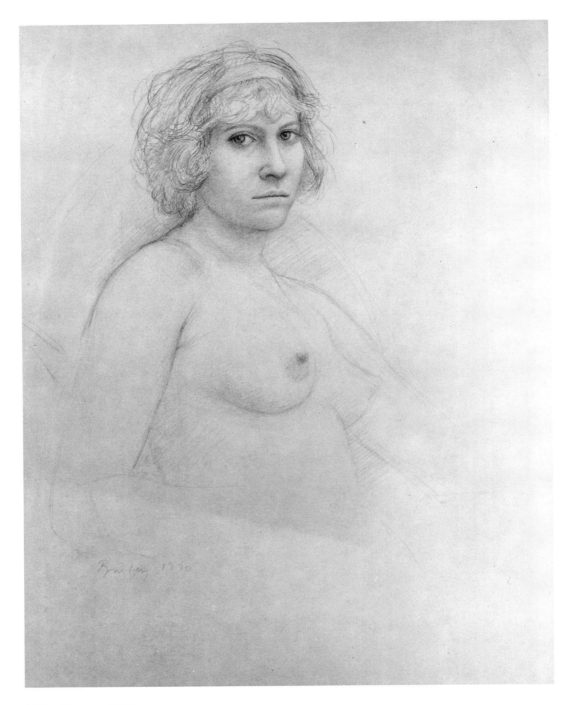

135. *Figure,* 1970

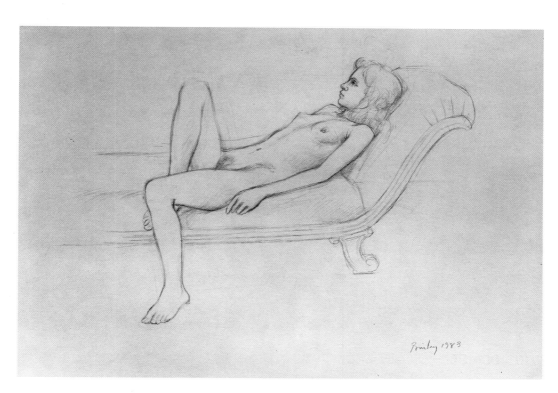

136. *Reclining figure,* 1983

137. *Girl with necklace,* 1977

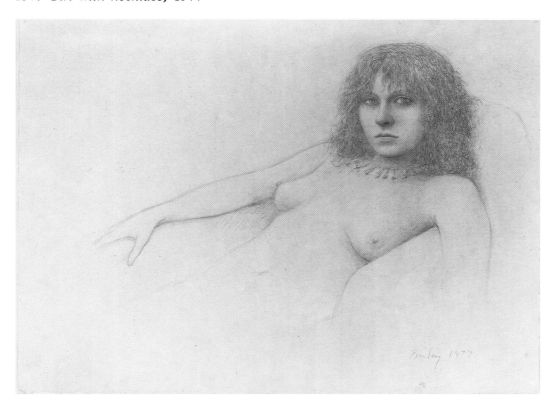

138. *Figure,* 1982

139. *Head,* 1975

140. *Figure,* 1983

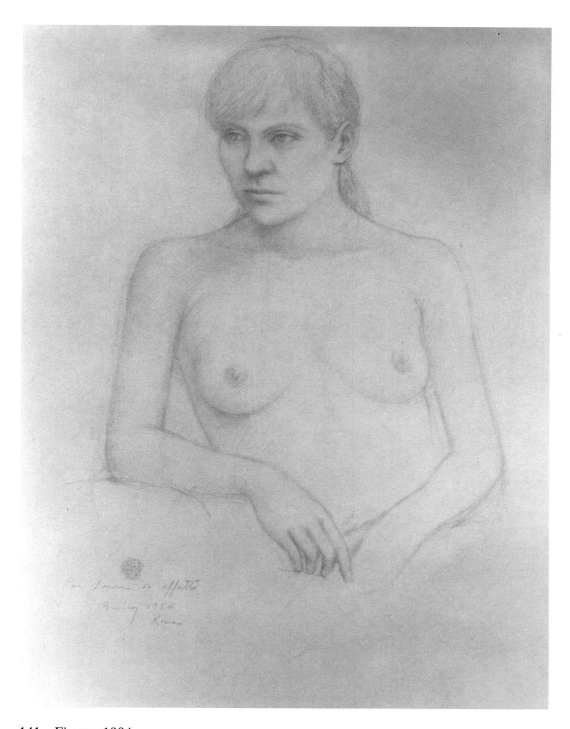

141. *Figure,* 1984

142. *Sleeping woman,* 1984

143. *Head,* 1982

144. *Girl with long hair,* 1985

158

145. *Head,* 1984

146. *Untitled still life,* 1986

160

147. *Untitled still life,* 1986

148. *Figure,* 1983

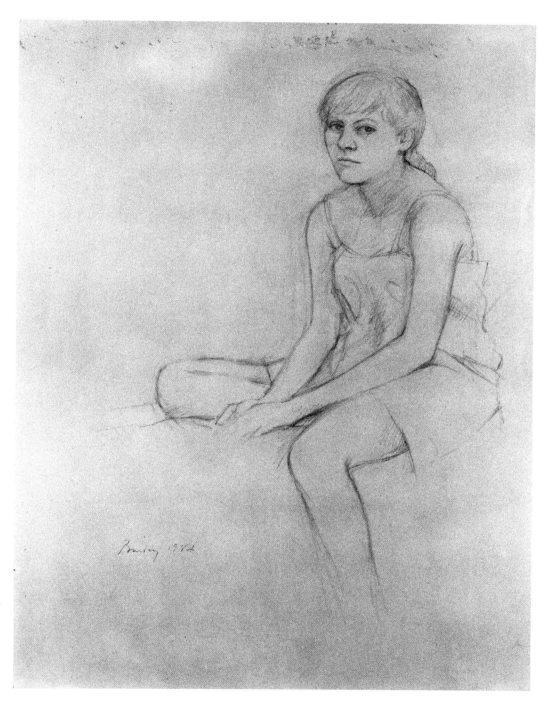

149. *Seated figure,* 1984

150. *Figure,* 1983

151. *Seated figure,* 1984

152. *Untitled figure,* 1984

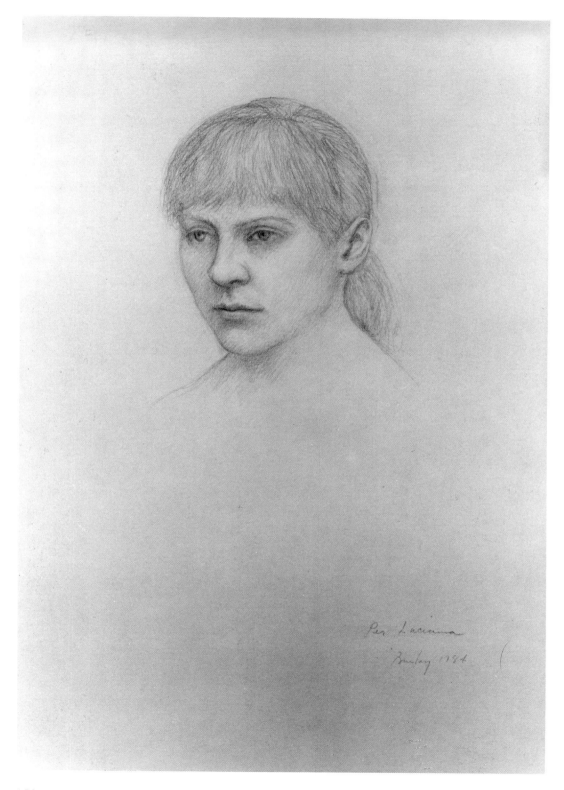

153. *Head,* 1984

154. *Untitled figure,* 1984

155. *Portrait,* 1987

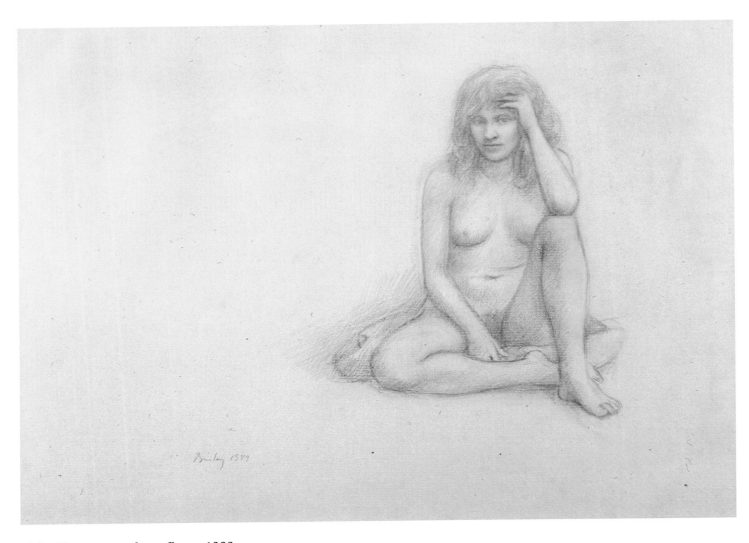

156. *Figure seated on floor,* 1989

157. *Reclining figure,* 1989

158. *Untitled still life,* 1987

159. *Untitled still life,* 1987

160. *Untitled still life,* 1988

174

161. *Untitled still life,* 1987

162. *Sleeping figure,* 1989

163. *Girl reclining,* 1989

LIST OF ILLUSTRATIONS

46. *Still life Rome,* 1976, 45 × 57½ in., oil on canvas, Neue Galerie der Stadt Aachen.

47. *Small Orvieto still life,* 1977, 25½ × 32 in., oil on canvas, Mr. and Mrs. John Berggruen Coll., San Francisco.

48. *Girl in white skirt,* 1977, 28¾ × 23½ in., oil on canvas, Mr. and Mrs. Daniel Halpern Coll., New York.

49. *Fratta,* 1978, 45 × 48 in., oil on canvas, Priv. Coll.

50. *Still life with rose wall and compote,* 1977, 40 × 48 in., oil on canvas, Hirschhorn Museum and Sculpture Garden, Washington, D.C.

51. *Grecian still life,* 1978, 42 × 50 in., oil on canvas, Pillsbury Family Coll., Fort Worth, Texas.

52. *Large Rome still life,* 1977, 52½ × 78 in., oil on canvas, Daniel and Barbara Fendrich Coll., Washington, D.C.

53. *Still life with red-brown wall,* 1978, 35 × 50 in., oil on canvas, Priv. Coll.

54. *Still life Manfroni,* 1978, 45 × 58 in., oil on canvas, Rose Art Museum, Brandeis University Coll., Waltham, Massachussets.

55. *Large umbrian still life,* 1978, 54 × 60 in., oil on canvas, St. Louis Art Museum.

56. *Piazza Fortebraccio,* 1981, 51 × 38 in., Gund Coll., Cambridge, Massachussets.

57. *Still life Torre Gentile,* 1979, 31¾ × 39½ in., oil on canvas, Priv. Coll., Turin.

58. *Perugina,* 1982, 72 × 50 in., oil on canvas, Mr. and Mrs. Alan J. Hruske Coll.

59. *Still life Montefalco,* 1979, 35 × 46⅜ in., oil on canvas, Priv. Coll., Turin.

60. *Still life Monte Migiana,* 1980, 54 × 60 in., oil on canvas, Pennsylvania Academy of Fine Arts, Philadelphia.

61. *Still life Bevagna,* 1980, 35 × 45⅜ in., oil on canvas, Del Drago Coll., Rome.

62. *Still life Castel Rigone,* 1980, 23½ × 28¾ in., oil on canvas, Priv. Coll.

63. *Still life Città di Castello,* 1980, 35 × 46¼ in., oil on canvas, Kronos Coll.

64. *Study for visitor,* 1980, 13 × 16 in., oil on canvas, Priv. Coll.

65. *Still life Monterchi,* 1981, 38 × 51 in., oil on canvas, Priv. Coll.

66. *Portrait of S,* 1980, 50 × 40 in., oil on canvas, University of Virginia Art Museum Coll., Charlottesville.

67. *Still life Norcia,* 1982, 50 × 40 in., oil on canvas, Priv. Coll.

68. *Still life Umbrian II,* 1982, 50 × 60 in., oil on canvas, Mr. and Mrs. James A. Fischer Coll.

69. *Still life Trevi,* 1982, 25½ × 21¼ in., oil on canvas, Priv. Coll.

70. *Still life Torre,* 1984, 45⅝ × 35⅛ in., oil on canvas, Priv. Coll., Stanford, California.

71. *Still life Trestina,* 1984, 23½ × 28½ in., oil on canvas, J. Goodman Coll., New York.

72. *Still life Genova,* 1984, 51 × 76¾ in., oil on canvas, Exxon Corporation Coll.

73. *Still life Galera,* 1982, 40 × 48 in., oil on canvas, Priv. Coll.

74. *Still life Pietralunga,* 1983, 40 × 50 in., oil on canvas, Joel Bernstein Coll.

75. *Still life Villa Aurelia,* 1983, 44 × 57½ in., oil on canvas, William Janss Coll.

76. *Still life Calzolaro,* 1983, 31¾ × 39½ in., oil on canvas, Priv. Coll., Palermo.

77. *Small figure,* 1977–83, 19¾ × 15¾ in., oil on canvas, Priv. Coll., New York.

78. *Still life Pisa,* 1984, 50 × 60 in., oil on canvas, Mr. and Mrs. Alan Tishman Coll., New York.

79. *Still life Paestum,* 1985, 51 × 63¾ in., oil on canvas, Jonathan Beare Coll., Los Angeles.

80. *Still life Hotel Raphael,* 1985, 40 × 50 in., oil on canvas, The Equitable Life Assurance Society of the U.S.A. Coll.

81. *Still life Hotel Locarno,* 1985, 30 × 36 in., oil on canvas, Wichita Art Museum, Kansas.

82. *Still life Pierle,* 1987, 55 × 65 in., oil on canvas, Priv. Coll.

83. *East rock,* 1987, 40 × 50 in., oil on canvas, Priv. Coll.

84. *Portrait of L,* 1986, 51 × 38 in., oil on canvas, Priv. Coll.

85. *Still life Noto,* 1986, 40 × 50 in., oil on canvas, Diane and David Goldsmith Coll., California.

86. *Duomo,* 1987, 60 × 50 in., oil on canvas, New Jersey State Museum, Trenton.

87. *Study for visitor,* 1988, 17⅞ × 22⅞ in., oil on canvas, Mr. and Mrs. Mark Strand Coll., Salt Lake City, Utah.

88. *Still life Civitella,* 1987, 55 × 65 in., oil on canvas, Jonathan Beare Coll., Los Angeles.

89. *Still life Bettona,* 1988, 39½ × 51½ in., oil on canvas, Priv. Coll.

90. *Looking east,* 1988, 51½ × 63 in., oil on canvas, Priv. Coll.

91. *Still life Verona,* 1988, 40 × 50 in., oil on canvas, Sidney and George Perutz Coll.

92. *Peck Street,* 1989, 50 × 60 in., oil on canvas, Robert Schoelkopf Gallery, New York.

93. *Paesaggio senese II,* 1989, 30 × 36 in., oil on canvas, Priv. Coll.

94. *Montalcino,* 1989, 51½ × 38½ in., oil on canvas, Priv. Coll., Rome.

95. *Still life Terontola,* 1988, 30⅛ × 36⅛ in., oil on canvas, Irvin Cohen Coll.

96. *Mensola,* 1989, 40 × 50 in., oil on canvas, Priv. Coll.

97. *Strada bianca,* 1990, 23½ × 28¾ in., oil on canvas, Galleria Il Gabbiano Coll., Rome.

98. *Pian del Voglio,* 1990, 60½ × 69½ in., oil on canvas, Galleria Il Gabbiano Coll., Rome.

99. *Small still life,* 1978, 9 × 11¾ in., casein on paper, Sandro Manzo Coll., Rome.

100. *Ginepro,* 1978, 12 × 16 in., casein on paper, Ford Bailey Coll.

101. *Ginepro,* 1978, 11⅞ × 15⅛ in., casein on paper, Sandra Bailey Coll.

102. *Ginepro n. 1,* 1979, 11¾ × 17¼ in., casein on paper, Priv. Coll., Rome.

103. *Ginepro n. 4,* 1980, 14 × 17 in., casein on paper, Priv. Coll., Rome.

104. *Ginepro n. 5,* 1980, 18 × 21 in., casein on paper, Regis Coll., Rome.

105. *Ginepro n. 6,* 1980, 13¾ × 19¾ in., casein on paper, Stanford Coll., California.

106. *Deruta,* 1983, 20 × 24 in., casein on paper, Priv. Coll.

107. *Still life Piazza San Francesco,* 1982, 18½ × 14 in., casein on paper, Rita Rich Coll.

108. *Pieroni,* 1981, 15 × 20 in., casein on paper, Priv. Coll.

109. *Montelovesco,* 1982, 14 × 17¼ in., casein on paper, Gregorio Rossi di Montelera Coll., Paris.

110. *Marsciano,* 1982, 17¼ × 14 in., casein on paper, Priv. Coll.

111. *Acquasparta,* 1987, 20 × 22¾ in., casein on paper, Priv. Coll.

112. *Castiglione,* 1983, 20 × 16 in., casein on paper.

113. *San Pancrazio,* 1984, 15 × 19¼ in., casein on paper, Bonitatibus Coll., Torino.

114. *Study,* 1985, 12¾ × 19 in., casein on paper, Blini Coll., Rome.

115. *San Liberato,* 1984, 15 × 20 in., casein on paper, Priv. Coll., New York.

116. *Still life Preggio,* 1986, 16 × 20 in., casein on paper, The Equitable Assurance Society of the USA Coll.

117. *Via Angelo Masina,* 1983, 16 × 20 in., casein on paper, Chemical Bank Coll., New York.

118. *Pergo,* 1987, 17 × 19¾ in., casein on paper, Priv. Coll.

119. *Still life Livorno,* 1987, 20⅝ × 25¼ in., casein on paper, Jerald Dillon Fessenden Coll., New York.

120. *Paesaggio senese,* 1989, 14½ × 18½ in., casein on paper, Alberto Ginobbi Coll., Rome.

121. *Still life Montecastelli,* 1988, 18 × 22 in., casein on paper, Priv. Coll.

122. *Untitled,* 1990, 18 × 22½ in., casein on paper, Galleria Il Gabbiano Coll., Rome.

123. Girl dressing, 1961, 7¼ × 11¼ in., wash drawing, Coll. the Artist.

124. *Back,* 1961, 7¼ × 11¼ in., silverpoint with white on rose ground, Coll. the Artist.

125. *Portrait,* 1961, 7¼ × 11¼ in., silverpoint with white on rose ground, Coll. the Artist.

126. *Figure,* 1984, 15 × 11 in., wash drawing, Il Gabbiano Coll., Rome.

127. *Figure,* 1984, 11 × 15 in., wash drawing, Husson Coll., Washington.

128. *Head,* 1984, 19 × 13 in., sanguine, Giorgio Soavi Coll., Milan.

129. *Study after Ingres,* 1961, 7 × 10 in., silverpoint with white, Coll. the Artist.

130. *Head,* 1961, pencil, Coll. the Artist.

131. *Seated figure,* 1970, 14 × 11 in., pencil, Coll. the Artist.

132. *Eggs and drapery,* 1961, 14 × 11 in., pencil, Priv. Coll.

133. *Seated figure,* 1974, 15 × 11¼ in., pencil, Priv. Coll.

134. *Eggs and drapery,* 1961, 14 × 11 in., pencil, Priv. Coll.

135. *Figure,* 1970, pencil, Priv. Coll.

136. *Reclining figure,* 1983, 13⅝ × 19¾ in., pencil, Priv. Coll.

137. *Girl with necklace,* 1977, 11 × 14 in., pencil, Mr. and Mrs. Daniel Halpern Coll., New York.

138. *Figure,* 1982, 14¾ × 10¾ in., pencil, Sandro Manzo Coll., Rome.

139. *Head,* 1975, 14¼ × 11 in., pencil, Mr. and Mrs. Mark Strand Coll.

140. *Figure,* 1983, 14¾ × 10¾ in., pencil, Sandro Manzo Coll., Rome.

141. *Figure,* 1984, 14¾ × 10¾ in., pencil, Laura Mazza Coll., Rome.

142. *Sleeping woman,* 1984, 13¼ × 19 in., pencil, Robert Schoelkopf Coll., New York.

143. *Head,* 1982, 15 × 11 in., pencil, Jane Schoelkopf Coll.

144. *Girl with long hair,* 1985, 30 × 22 in., pencil, Priv. Coll.

145. *Head,* 1984, 13 × 9½ in., pencil, Marisa Volpi Coll., Rome.

146. *Untitled still life,* 1986, 18 × 15 in., pencil, Priv. Coll.

147. *Untitled still life,* 1986, 18 × 15 in., pencil, Priv. Coll.

148. *Figure,* 1983, 11 × 15 in., pencil, Alfredo de Marzio Coll., New York.

149. *Seated figure,* 1984, 14½ × 10½ in., pencil, Galleria Il Gabbiano, Rome.

150. *Figure,* 1983, 19½ × 14 in., pencil, Pierre Levai Coll., New York.

151. *Seated figure,* 1984, 13 × 19 in., pencil, Del Vecchio Coll., Rome.

152. *Untitled figure,* 1984, 15 × 11 in., pencil, Galleria Il Gabbiano, Rome.

153. *Head,* 1984, 14¾ × 10¾ in., pencil, Luciana Alessi Coll., Rome.

154. *Untitled figure,* 1984, 19¾ × 13¾ in., pencil, Galleria Il Gabbiano Coll., Rome.

155. *Portrait,* 1987, 27¼ × 19¾ in., pencil, Gregorio Rossi di Montelera Coll., Parigi.

156. *Figure seated on floor,* 1989, 19½ × 26 in., pencil, Priv. Coll.

157. *Reclining figure,* 1989, 19½ × 26 in., pencil, Priv. Coll.

158. *Untitled still life,* 1987, 19 × 26½ in., pencil, Priv. Coll.

159. *Untitled still life,* 1987, 19 × 26 in., pencil, Priv. Coll.

160. *Untitled still life,* 1988, 19 × 26½ in., pencil, Priv. Coll.

161. *Untitled still life,* 1987, 19 × 26 in., pencil, Priv. Coll.

162. *Sleeping figure,* 1989, 19½ × 26 in., pencil, Priv. Coll.

163. *Girl reclining,* 1989, 19½ × 26½ in., pencil, Priv. Coll.

BIOGRAPHY

Born: November 17, 1930, Council Bluffs, Iowa.
Residence: New Haven, Connecticut and Umbertide, Italy.

EDUCATION

University of Kansas, School of Fine Arts, 1948–51.
Yale University, School of Art, B.F.A. 1955.
Yale University, School of Art, M.F.A. 1957.

AWARDS

1955

Alice Kimball English Traveling Fellowship.

1958

First Prize in Painting, Boston Arts Festival.

1960

American Specialist Grant, travel in Southeast Asia.

1965

Guggenheim Fellowship in Painting.

1975

Igram-Merrill Foundation Grant for Painting.

1976–77

Visiting Artist, American Academy in Rome.

1985

Yale Arts Medal for Distinguished Contribution in Painting.

1986

Elected Member of the American Academy and Institute of Arts and Letters.

1987

Honorary Doctor of Humanities, University of Utah.

TEACHING

1957–62

School of Art, Yale University.

1962–69

Indiana University.

1969–79

Professor of Art, School of Art, Yale University.

1974–75

Dean of the School of Art, Yale University.

From 1979

Kingman Brewster Professor of Art, School of Art, Yale University.

EXHIBITIONS

ONE-MAN EXHIBITIONS

1956
Robert Hull Fleming Museum, University of Vermont, Burlington.

1957
Kanegis Gallery, Boston.

1958
Kanegis Gallery, Boston.

1961
Kanegis Gallery, Boston.

1963
Indiana University Art Museum, Indiana University.

1967
Kansas City Art Institute, Kansas City, Missouri.

1968
Robert Schoelkopf Gallery, New York.

1969
Nasson College, Springvale, Maine.

1971
Robert Schoelkopf Gallery, New York.

1972
Queens College, City University of New York, Flushing. Tyler School of Art, Temple University, Philadelphia. University of Connecticut, Storrs.

1973
Galleria il Fante di Spade, Rome. Galleria Dei Lanzi, Milan. Galleria La Parisina, Turin.

1974
Robert Schoelkopf Gallery, New York.

1975
Polk Museum, Lakeland, Florida. Exhibition traveled to Ft. Lauderdale, Florida.

1976
Dart Gallery, Chicago.

1978
Galerie Claude Bernard, Parigi.

1979
Robert Schoelkopf Gallery, New York. Fendrick Gallery, Washington, D.C.

1980
Galleria il Gabbiano, Rome.

1982
Robert Schoelkopf Gallery, New York.

1983
Meadows Gallery, Southern Methodist University, Dallas, Texas.

1984
American Academy in Rome.

1985
Galleria il Gabbiano, Rome.

1986
Robert Schoelkopf Gallery, New York.

1987
FIAC Paris, Grand Palais (Galleria Il Gabbiano, Rome).

1987
University Art Galleries, Wright State University, Dayton, Ohio.

1988
John Berggruen Gallery, San Francisco.

1988
Rhode Island School of Design, Providence.

1989
Center for Financial Studies, Fairfield, Connecticut; Fairfield Artist of the Year.

Bailey in the Studio in Weir Hall, Yale University, 1971

GROUP EXHIBITIONS

1957

"Selection 1957," Institute of Contemporary Art, Boston.

1959

"New Talent 1959," Art in America, New York.

1960

"View of 1960," Institute of Contemporary Art, Boston.

"Image and Idea," Museum of Contemporary Art, Houston, Texas.

1961

"Contemporary American Painting and Sculpture," University of Illinois, Champaign-Urbana.

1962

"Five New England Artists," Silvermine Guild Center for the Arts, New Canaan, Connecticut.

1963

"Contemporary American and Italian Drawings," D'Arcy Gallery, New York. "Graphics 1963," University of Kentucky.

1964

"The Figure," Drawings 1500–1964, University of Iowa Art Museum.

1967

"Art on Paper," Weatherspoon Gallery, University of North Carolina, Greensboro.

1968

"The Big Figure," Wilcox Gallery, Swarthmore College, Swarthmore, Pennsylvania.
"Realism Now," Vassar College Art Gallery, Vassar College, Poughkeepsie, New York.

"Drawings by Six Artists," State University of New York at Cortland.

1969

"Drawings U.S.A. 1968," St. Paul Art Center, St. Paul, Minnesota.

"New Realism 1970," St. Cloud State College, St. Cloud, Minnesota.

1970

"22 Realists," Whitney Museum of American Art, New York. "Childe Hassam Purchase Exhibition," American Academy and Institute of Arts and Letters, New York.

1971

"Childe Hassam Purchase Exhibition," The American Academy and Institute of Arts and Letters, New York. "Realist Painting," Florida State University, Tallahassee. Exhibition traveled to University of New Mexico, Albuquerque.

1972

"Five Figurative Artists," Kansas City Art Institute, Kansas City, Missouri. Exhibition traveled to Weatherspoon Gallery, University of North Carolina, Greensboro; Butler Institute of American Art, Youngstown, Ohio.
"Realism" organized by The American Federation of the Arts, Rhode Island School of Design, Providence, Rhode Island.
"Confronto sulla realtà," Riccione.

1973

"Realist Revival," New York Cultural Center, New York.

1974

"Living American Artists and the Figure," Pennsylvania State University, University Park.
"Seven Realists," Yale University Art Gallery, New Haven, Connecticut.

"Soft Line Drawing," Frederick Gallery, Washington, D.C.

1975

"The Figure in Recent American Painting," St. John's University, Jamaica, New York.
"Three Centuries of the American Nude," New York Cultural Center, New York.
"William Bailey and Brice Marden: Recent Prints," Knoedler Graphics, New York.

1976

"America, the Third Century," Underwriters, Mobile Oil, The Corcoran Gallery of Art, Washington, D.C.

1. *Bailey,* University of Kansas,
   1950

2-3-4-5. *Bailey in his studio,*
   Paris, 1965—66

1976

"American Figure Drawings," Lehigh University, Bethlehem, Pennsylvania.

1977

"Biennale Internationale," Palazzo Strozzi, Florence. "William Bailey and Costantino Nivola," American Academy in Rome.

1978

"American Academy in Rome: Five Painters," Union Carbide Building, New York.
"Salon de Mai," Paris.
"Selected 20th Century American Nudes," Harold Reed Gallery, New York.
"The Other Realism," Figure drawings, Ben Shahn Gallery, William Patterson College, Wayne, New Jersey.

1979

"American Painting of the 60s and 70s. The Real, The Ideal, The Fantastic," Whitney Museum of American Art, New York.
"Artists Choose: Figurative/Realist Art," Artist's Choice Museum, New York.
"Drawings 1979," Landmark Gallery, New York.

1980

"The Figurative Tradition," Whitney Museum of American Art, New York.
"Still Life Today," Goddard-Riverside Community Center, New York.

1981

"American Painting 1930–1980," Haus der Kunst, Munich, West Germany. Organized by the Whitney Museum of American Art, New York.
"Contemporary American Realism Since 1960," Pennsylvania Academy of the Fine Arts, Philadelphia. Exhibition traveled to Oakland Museum, California; Virginia Museum of Fine Arts, Richmond. Exhibition traveled abroad to Portugal, Germany, and Holland 1982–83.
"Contemporary Artists," The Cleveland Museum of Art, Ohio.
"The Image in American Painting and Sculpture 1950–1980," Akron Art Museum, Ohio.
"Joseph Albers: His Art and Influence," Montclair Art Museum, New Jersey.

"Mantegna to Rauschenberg: Six Centuries of Prints," Babcock Gallery, New York.
"Real, Really Real and Super Real," San Antonio Museum of Art, Texas. Exhibition traveled to Tucson Museum of Art, Arizona; Museum of Art, Carnegie Institute, Pittsburgh.
"20 Artists: Yale School of Art 1950–1970," Yale University Art Gallery, New Haven.
"The Whitney Biennial," Whitney Museum of American Art, New York.
"Contemporary Figure Drawings," Robert Schoelkopf Gallery, New York.

1982

"Paintings and Sculpture by Candidates for Art Awards," The American Academy and Institute of Arts and Letters, New York.
"Perspectives on Contemporary American Realism: Works of Art on Paper from the Collection of Jalane and Richard Davidson," Pennsylvania Academy of the Fine Arts, Philadelphia. Exhibition traveled to The Art Institute of Chicago.
"A Private Vision: Contemporary Art from the Graham Gund Collection," Museum of Fine Arts, Boston.

1983

"American Still Life: 1945–1983," Contemporary Arts Museum, Houston, Texas. Exhibition traveled to the Albright-Knox Art Gallery, Buffalo, New York; Columbus Museum of Art, Ohio; Neuberger Museum, State University of New York at Purchase; Portland Art Museum, Oregon.
"A Heritage Renewed: Representational Drawing Today," University Art Museum, University of California, Santa Barbara. Exhibition traveled to Oklahoma Art Center, Oklahoma; Elvehjem Museum of Art, University of Wisconsin, Madison; Colorado Springs Fine Arts Center, Colorado.
"Connecticut Painters: 7 Plus 7 Plus 7," Wadsworth Atheneum, Hartford, Connecticut.
"Live from Connecticut," Whitney Museum of Art, Stamford, Connecticut.
"Realistic Directions," Zoller Gallery, Pennsylvania State University.

1984

"Invitational Drawing Exhibition," Art and Architecture Gallery, University of Tennessee, Knoxville.

"New York Realism: Small Works and Preliminary Sketches," College of the Mainland Art Gallery, Texas City, Texas.
"Print Acquisitions 1974–1984," Whitney Museum of American Art, New York.
"Recent American Still Life Painting," Robert Schoelkopf Gallery, New York.
"Realism: Drawings and Watercolors," USF Galleries, University of Southern Florida, Tampa.
"Two Presses. Two Processes," Bucknell University, Pennsylvania.
"L'immagine e il suo doppio," Palazzo Bagatti Valsecchi, Milan.
"Mark Strand Collection," University of Utah, Salt Lake City.

1985

"American Art Today: Still Life," Florida International University, Miami.
"A Decade of American Realism: 1975–1985," Wichita Art Museum, Kansas.
"Focus on Realism: Selections from the Collection of Glenn C. Janss, Boise Gallery of Art, Idaho. "Visiting Artists," Kansas City Art Institute, Kansas City, Missouri.
"Recent American Portraiture," Robert Schoelkopf Gallery, New York.
"Contemporary American Still Life," One Penn Plaza, New York.
"Umbria; Americans Painting in Italy," Gallery North, Setauket, New York.

1985–86

"American Realism: Twentieth Century Drawings and Watercolors from the Collection of Glenn C. Janss," San Francisco Museum of Modern Art. Exhibition traveled to DeCordova and Dana Museum, Lincoln, Massachusetts; Huntington Art Gallery, University of Texas, Austin; Mary and Leigh Block Gallery, Northwestern University, Evanston, Illinois; Museum of Art, Williams College, Williamstown, Massachusetts; Akron Art Museum, Ohio; Madison Art Center, Wisconsin.

1986

"American Drawings: Realism/Idealism," Jane Haslem Gallery, Washington, D.C.
"Exhibition of Work by Newly Elected Members and Recipients of Awards," The American Academy and Institute of Arts and Letters, New York.
"American Academy and Institute of Arts and Letters," New York.

6. *Bailey and his son Ford,*
   Todi, 1978

7. *The Studio,*
   Schioppe di Migianella,
   Umbria, 1990

8. *The House and Studio,*
   Schioppe di Migianella, 1990

9. *Bailey and his doughter Alix in*
   front of his wife Sandra
   Stone's studio, Schioppe di
   Migianella, 1987

10. *Ford, Alix, Sandra,*
    William Bailey at
    Schioppe di Migianella,
    Umbria, 1973

6

7

8

9

10

1987

"The Homecoming," Iowa Art Council and the Gallery of Art, University of Northern Iowa, Cedar Falls.
"Faculty Show," Yale University School of Art, Yale University, New Haven, Connecticut.
"Realism Today," National Academy of Design, New York.

1988

"Chicago Collects: Selections from the Collection of Dr. Eugene A. Solow," Chauncey McCormick Gallery.
"A Decade of American Drawing 1980–1989," Daniel Weinberg Gallery, Los Angeles. "Drawings," Anchorage Museum of History and Art, Anchorage, Alaska.
"Bailey - Kopp - Theimer Tre artisti stranieri in Italia," Istituto Nazionale per la Grafica, Calcografia – Rome.

1989

"Paintings and Works on Paper," John Berggruen Gallery, San Francisco.
"Drawing: Points of View," Belk Art Gallery, Western Carolina University.

1990

"Underneath It All; Works on Paper by Selected Artists," Maxwell Davidson Gallery, New York.
"Objects Observed: Contemporary Still Life," Gallery Henoch, New York. Feb. 13 – Mar. 10, 1990.
"Benefit exhibition for AIDS Research," Daniel Weinberg Gallery, Los Angeles.
FIAC Paris, Grand Palais (Galleria Il Gabbiano, Rome).

PUBLIC COLLECTIONS

Arkansas Arts Center, Little Rock.
The Art Institute of Chicago.
Chemical Bank, New York.
Des Moines Art Center, Iowa.
Equitable Real Estate Group, Inc., New York.
Estee Lauder, Inc., New York.
Exxon Corporation, New York.
General Mills Corporation, Minneapolis, Minnesota.
The Hirshhorn Museum and Sculpture Garden, Smithsonian Institution, Washington, D.C.
Indiana University Art Museum, Bloomington.
J.B. Speed Museum, Louisville, Kentucky.
J. Henry Schroder Banking Corporation, New York.
Kresge Art Museum, Michigan State University, East Lansing.
Lehman Brothers Shearson American Express, New York.
Montclair Art Museum, New Jersey.
Museum of Art, Duke University, Durham, North Carolina.
Museum of Art of Ogunquit, Ogunquit, Maine.
Museum of Fine Arts, Boston.
The Museum of Modern Art, New York.
National Museum of American Art, Smithsonian Institution, Washington, D.C.
New Jersey State Museum, Trenton.
The New York Times, New York.
Ing. C. Olivetti & C., S.p.A., Ivrea, Italy.
Pennsylvania Academy of the Fine Arts, Philadelphia.
Pennsylvania State University, University Park.
Rose Art Museum, Brandeis University, Waltham, Massachusetts.
St. Louis Art Museum, Missouri.
Sheldon Swope Art Gallery, Terre Haute, Indiana.
Städtisches/Suermondt-Ludwig-Museum, Aachen, West Germany.
State University of New York at Cortland.
University of Kentucky, Lexington.
University of Massachusetts, Amherst.
University of New Mexico, Albuquerque.
University of Virginia Art Museum, Charlottesville.
Weatherspoon Art Gallery, University of North Carolina, Greensboro.
Whitney Museum of American Art, New York.
Wichita Art Museum, Kansas.
William Benton Museum of Art, University of Connecticut, Storrs.
Yale University Art Gallery, New Haven.

11. *Bailey and Robert Schoelkopf at the opening of his exhibition at Galerie Claude Bernard,* Paris, 1978

12. *William and Sandra Bailey with Sandro Manzo Fiac,* Paris, 1987

13. *Bailey with Sandro Manzo at Schioppe di Migianella,* Umbria, 1990

14. *Bailey with Riccardo Tommasi Ferroni at Galleria Il Gabbiano,* Rome, 1981

15. *Bailey and John Hollander in front of the American Academy and Institute of Arts and Letters,* New York, 1986

16. *Bailey and Andrew Forge at Schioppe di Migianella,* 1989

13

11

14

15

12

16

SELECTED BIBLIOGRAPHY

EXHIBITION CATALOGUES

Selection 1957. Text by Thomas M. Messer. Boston: Institute of Contemporary Art, 1957.

Contemporary American Painting and Sculpture. Text by Allen S. Weller. Urbana, Illinois: Krannert Art Museum, 1961.

Graphics 1963. Preface by Edward W. Rannels. Lexington, Kentucky: University of Kentucky Art Gallery, 1963.

Realism Now. Text by Linda Nochlin. Poughkeepsie, New York: Vassar College Art Gallery, 1968.

22 Realists. Text by James K. Monte. New York: Whitney Museum of American Art, 1970.

Becker, Ludwig. *Neue Galerie der Stadt Aachen: Der Bestand 72* [catalogue of the collection]. Aachen, West Germany: the museum, 1972.

William Bailey. Essay by Ugheta Fitzgerald ("Alcune note sulla pittura di William Bailey.") Rome: Galleria il Fante di Spade, 1973.

American Poster 1945–75. Text by Margaret Cogswell. Washington, D.C.: Corcoran Gallery of Art, 1975.

Seven Realists. Preface by Alan Shestack, essay on William Bailey by A[nne] M[cAuley]. New Haven, Connecticut: Yale University Art Gallery, 1974.

Connecticut Painting, Drawing and Sculpture 78. Text by Virginia Mann Haggin. New Haven, Connecticut: University of Bridgeport, 1978.

William Bailey: Peintures. Essays by Hilton Kramer and Jean Paget. Paris: Galerie Claude Bernard, 1978.

William Bailey: Recent Paintings. Introduction by Mark Strand. New York: Robert Schoelkopf Gallery, 1979.

Still-Life and the Figure by William Bailey. Text by David Tannous. Washington, D.C.: Frendrick Gallery, 1979.

William Bailey: Paintings and drawings. Text by Alberto Moravia and Mark Strand. Rome: Galleria Il Gabbiano, 1980.

William Bailey: Recent Paintings. Introduction by John Hollander. New York: Robert Schoelkopf Gallery, 1982.

L'immagine e il suo Doppio. Text by Floriano De Santi. Milan: Palazzo Bagatti Valsecchi, 1984.

Invitational Drawing Exhibition. Text by Sam Yates. Knoxville: University of Tennessee, 1984.

Parasol and Simca: Two Presses/Two Processes. Text by Lizbeth Marano. Lewisburg, Pennsylvania: Center Gallery of Bucknell University, 1984.

American Art Today: Still Life. Text by Carter Ratcliff. Miami: Florida International University, 1985.

American Realism: Twentieth Century Drawings and Watercolors from the Collection of Glenn C. Janns. Text by Alvin Martin. San Francisco Museum of Modern Art, 1985.

Nudi di William Bailey. Text by Giorgio Soavi. Rome: Galleria Il Gabbiano, 1985.

William Bailey: Recent Paintings. Introduction by Andrew Forge. New York: Robert Schoelkopf Gallery, 1986.

William Bailey: Recent paintings and drawings. Text by Robert Flynn Johnson. San Francisco: John Berggruen Gallery, 1988.

"Bailey-Kopp-Theimer. Tre Artisti stranieri in Italia." Introduction by Giuliano Briganti and text by Marisa Volpi. Rome: De Luca, 1988.

BOOKS

American Still Life: 1945–83. Text by Linda L. Cathcart. New York: Harper & Row in conjunction with the Contemporary Arts Museum, Houston, Texas, 1983.

Disegni e tempere di William Bailey. Text by Andrew Forge. Milan: Olivetti, 1987.

Arthur, John. *Realist Drawings and Watercolors*. Boston: New York Graphic Society, 1980.

Goodyear, Jr., Frank H. *Contemporary American Realism Since 1960*. Boston: New York Graphic Society in association with the Pennsylvania Academy of the Fine Arts, 1981.

Haim, Nadine. *Peintures aux Fourneaux*. Paris: Flammarion, 1985.

Kahmen, Volker. *Erotic Art Today*. Greenwich, Connecticut: New York Graphic Society, 1972.

—. *The Age of the Avant-Garde: An Art Chronicle of 1956–1972*. New York: Farrar, Straus and Giroux, 1973.

Kultermann, Udo. *The New Painting*. Rev. ed. Boulder, Colorado: Westview Press, 1977.

Sager, Peter. *Neue Formen des Realismus*. Cologne: Verlag M. DuMont Schauberg, 1973.

Strand, Mark, ed. *Art of the Real: Nine American Figurative Painters*.

17. *The Studio in Weir Hall,* Yale University, 1972

18. *The Studio at Schioppe di Migianella,* Umbria, 1990

19. *The Studio at Schioppe di Migianella,* Umbria, 1986

20. *The Studio on State Street,* New Haven, Connecticut, 1988

21. *The Studio at Schioppe di Migianella,* Umbria, 1988

22. *The Studio on Peck Street,* New Haven, Connecticut, 1989

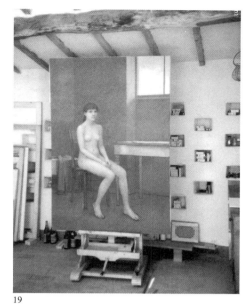

19

17

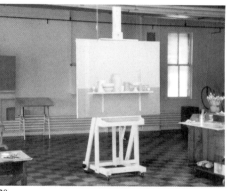

20

21

18

22

Foreword by Robert Hughes. New York: Clarkson N. Potter, Inc., 1983.

Strand, Mark. *William Bailey.* New York: Harry N. Abrams, Inc., 1987.

PERIODICAL AND NEWSPAPER ARTICLES

Alexandre, Phil. "William Bailey: The State of the Artist." *The Kenyon Journal,* May 1986, pp. 6–11.

Almansi, Guido. "Trittico per l'Italia." *La Repubblica* (Rome), March 12, 1988.

Apuleo, Vito. "William Bailey: Astratta Classicità." *Il Messaggero* (Rome), March 19, 1985.

"Artists Project, William Bailey." *Artforum,* September 1987.

Atner, Alan G. "Art." *Chicago Tribune,* April 3, 1983, arts and books section, pp. 16–17.

Bass, Ruth. "The illusion of Reality." *Art News,* vol. 80, no. 10 (Dec. 1981), pp. 78–81.

Bernardi, Marziano. "La Pittura e i Segni." *La Stampa* (Torino), Jan. 10, 1974, p. 7.

Bilardello, Enzo. "William Bailey." *Il Corriere della Sera* (Rome), Jan. 31, 1981.

B[rown], G[ordon]. "In the Galleries." *Arts Magazine,* vol. 42, no. 2 (Nov. 1971), p. 72.

C[ampbell], L[awrence]. "Reviews and Previews." *Art News,* vol. 70, no. 7, (Nov. 1971), p. 12.

Clair, Jean. "Il Ritorno della Natura Morta." *Casa Vogue,* Sept. 1981, pp. 352–55.

Davis, Douglas. "Mixed Marriages of Art." *Newsweek,* vol. 97, no. 11 (March 16, 1981), p. 71.

Diwan, Fiona. "Il Momento dei Nuovi Eclettici: I Tritatutto." *Panorama* (Milan), Sept. 6, 1982, pp. 82–86.

Dragone, Angelo. "Mostre d'Arte." *Stampa Sera* (Torino), Jan. 11, 1974.

Evett, Kenneth. "Academic Question." *The New Republic,* vol. 172, no. 7 (Feb. 15, 1975), pp. 30–31.

Filler, Martin. "Qu'est-ce qu'est Américain dans l'Architecture Américain?" *Paris Vogue,* April 19, 1982, pp. 222–23.

Forgey, Benjamin. "Painting the Familiar." *Washington Star* (Washington, D.C.), April 15, 1979.

French-Frazier, Nina. "William Bailey." *Arts Magazine,* vol. 53, no. 8 (April 1979), p. 9.

Gibson, Eric. "New York." *Art International,* vol. 22, no. 10 (March 1979), p. 49.

—. "American Still Life." *The New Criterion,* vol. 3, no. 2 (Oct. 1984), pp. 70–75.

Glueck, Grace. "Previews." *Art in America,* vol. 59 (March 1971), p. 45.

—. "Art: American Still Life with the Accent on Life." *The New York Times,* July 20, 1984.

—. "American Realism Since 1960: Beyond the Perfect Green Pea." *Portfolio Magazine,* Nov.–Dec. 1981, p. 72.

Gruen, John. "William Bailey: Mystery and Mastery." *Art News,* vol. 78, no. 9 (Nov. 1979), pp. 140–43, 145.

G[uiliano], C[harles]. "In the Galleries." *Arts Magazine,* vol. 42, no. 5 (March 1968), p. 60.

Henry, Gerrit. "A Preference for the Perfect." *Art News,* vol. 78, no. 4 (April 1979), p. 145.

—. "Recent American Still Life Painting." *Art News,* vol. 85, no. 3 (March 1985), p. 144.

—. "William Bailey at Schoelkopf." *Art in America,* vol. 75, no. 3 (March 1987), p. 140.

Hollander, John. "Artist's Dialogue: William Bailey, An Extreme and Abstract Clarity." *Architectural Digest,* Dec. 1986, pp. 44, 48–50.

Hughes, Robert. "The Realist as Corn God." *Time,* Jan. 31, 1972, pp. 50–55.

Jürgen-Fischer, Klaus. "Neuer Naturalismus." *Das Kunstwerk,* vol. 23, no. 5–6 (Feb.–March 1970), pp. 3–34.

Kohen, Helen L. "Still Life Paintings that will Take Your Breath Away." *Miami Herald,* Jan. 20, 1985.

Kramer, Hilton. "Form, Fantasy, and the Nude." *The New York Times,* Feb. 11, 1968, p. D25.

—. "Dear Reader, Worry No More." *The New York Times,* Feb. 15, 1970, sect. 2, p. 23.

—. "William Bailey and the Artifice of Realism." *The New York Times,* Oct. 31, 1971, sect. 2, p. 21.

—. "Extreme Cross Purposes." *The New York Times,* Dec. 10, 1972, sect. 2, p. 27.

—, "Realism: The Painting is Fiction Enough." *The New York Times,* April 28, 1974, sect. 2, p. 19.

—. "Art: William Bailey Still Lifes." *The New York Times,* Oct. 26, 1974, p. 25.

—. "Art: Stuart Davis and William Bailey." *The New York Times,* Jan. 12, 1979, p. C14.

—. "Art View: The Return of the Realists and a New Battle Shaping Up." *The New York Times,* Oct. 25, 1981, sect. 2, pp. 1–35.

Kutner, Janet. "Quiet Authority." *Dallas Morning News,* March 23, 1983, sect. C, pp. 1–3.

Laderman, Gabriel. "Unconventional Realists." *Artforum,* vol. 6, no. 3 (Nov. 1967), pp. 42–46.

Lanes, Jerold. "Review." *Burlington Magazine,* March 1968, p. 170.

—. "Problems of Representation: Are We Asking the Right Questions?" *Artforum,* Jan. 1972, pp. 60–62.

Lipman, Jean, ed. "New Talent 1959." *Art in America,* vol. 47, no. 1 (Spring 1959), p. 48.

Lubell, Ellen. "An Air of Serenity." *Soho Weekly News,* Jan. 18, 1979.

"Maestri del Silenzio." *Arte* (Milan), April 1985.

Marvel, Bill. "More Credible Than Realistic." *Dallas Times Herald,* March 9, 1983.

Mazars, Pierre. "Silence! Peinture." *Le Figaro* (Paris), April 14, 1978, p. 22.

Micacchi, Dario. "Realismo tradizionale nelle Opere di William Bailey." *L'Unità* (Rome), Feb. 24, 1973.

—. "Oggetti nuovi nella luce dell'antica Italia." *L'Unità* (Rome), Dec. 5, 1980.

Morosini, Duilio. "Bailey e il Realismo Classico." *Paese Sera* (Rome), Feb. 17, 1973, p. 10.

Navrozov, Andrei. "William Bailey." *Art and Antiques,* Oct. 1986, pp. 57–59.

Nemser, Cindy. "Representational Painting in 1971: A New Synthesis." *Arts Magazine,* vol. 46 (Dec. 1971), pp. 41–46.

Oersman, Janice C. "Still Life Today." *Arts Magazine,* vol. 57 (Dec. 1982), pp. 111–15.

Ouvaroff, I. E. "Quartetto Tacet." *The Yale Literary Magazine,* vol. 149, no. 1 (1981), pp. 8–13.

Perl, Jed. "William Bailey's Poetic Realism." *Columbia Daily Spectator,* Nov. 5, 1971, p. 4.

—. "The Life of the Object: Still Life Painting Today." *Arts Magazine,* vol. 52 (Dec. 1977), pp. 27–28.

P[errault], J[ohn]. "Reviews and Previews." *Art News,* vol. 67, no. 2 (April 1968), p. 9.

Plazi, Giles. "William Bailey." *Quotidien Paris,* March 28, 1978, p. 18.

Richard, Paul. "Clean, Fine, and Moving: The Still Life before the Storm." *Washington Post,* April 14, 1979.

Russell, John. "Recent Paintings by William Bailey." *The New York Times,* April 23, 1982, p. C22.

—. "Art: William Bailey." *The New York Times,* Nov. 28, 1986, p. C22.

Schjeldahl, Peter. "Realism — A retreat to the Fundamentals?" *The New York Times,* Dec. 24, 1972, sect. 2, p. 25.

Smith, Roberta. "Tempus Fidget." *Village Voice,* April 20, 1982, p. 89.

Soavi, Giorgio. "Figure." *Epoca* (Rome), May 4, 1984, p. 98.

Stevens, Mark. "Art Imitates Life: The Revival of Realism."

Newsweek, vol. 99, no. 23 (June 7, 1982), pp. 64–70 [cover story].

Tillim, Sidney. "The Reception of Figurative Art: Notes on a General Misunderstanding." *Artforum,* vol. 7 (Feb. 1969), pp. 30–33.

Trombadori, Antonello. "Nature morte e risuscitate." *Europeo,* Feb. 9, 1981, p. 70.

Trucchi, Lorenza. "Bailey al Fante di Spade." *Momento Sera* (Rome), Feb. 16, 1973.

"Weg von der Weihnachtsausstellung: *Spiegel*-Gespräch mit dem Dokumenta-Generalsekretär Harald Szeemann." *Der Spiegel,* April 12, 1971, p. 166.

White, Edmund. "Realism." *Saturday Review of the Arts,* vol. 1, no. 2 (Feb. 1973), p. 57.

Wolff, Theodore F. "Drawings from the Famous and the Promising." *Christian Science Monitor,* Jan. 20, 1988.

Zimmer, William. "Crockery, From a Painters Perspective." *The New York Times,* Nov. 28, 1986.

"Rutgers Museum Seeks to Give Prints Their Due," *The New York Times,* July 24, 1983, New Jersey section. *Times,* Dec. 24, 1979, sect 2. p. 25.

BOOKS ILLUSTRATED

Eighty Poems of Antonio Machado. Illustrations by William Bailey. New York: Las Americas, 1958.

A Lost Lady. Willa Cather. Illustrations by William Bailey. New York: The Limited Editions Club, 1983.

Agenda Olivetti. William Bailey. Milan: Olivetti, 1987.

23-24. *Bailey viewing color proofs for this book with Paola Gribaudo at Schioppe di Migianella,* 1990

DATE DUE

DATE DUE			
JAN 1 2 1999			
GAYLORD			PRINTED IN U.S.A.